Charles E. Poole

Is Life Fair?

Good Words for Hard Times

2nd Edition

To Our Parents

Hazel Wommack Smith
Joseph Daniel Smith
Charlie Cammack Poole
Olif Hubert Poole (*in memoriam*)

They taught us God's good words for life's hard times.

Charles E. Poole

Is Life Fair?

Good Words for Hard Times

2nd Edition

SMYTH&HELWYS
PUBLISHING, INCORPORATED MACON, GEORGIA

SMYTH&
HELWYS

Smyth & Helwys Publishing, Inc.
6316 Peake Road
Macon, Georgia 31210-3960
1-800-747-3016
©1996, 1999 by Smyth & Helwys Publishing
All right reserved.
First edition 1996.
Second edition 1999.
Printed in the United States of America.

Charles E. Poole

The paper used in this publication meets the minimum requirements
of American National Standard for Information
Sciences—Permanence of Paper for Printed Library Materials.
ANSI Z39.48–1984. (alk. paper)

Library of Congress Cataloging-in-Publication Data

Poole, Charles E.
     Is life fair?: good words for hard times : 2nd edition/
     Charles E. Poole.
     pp.   cm.
     1. Baptists—Sermons. 2. Sermons, American. I. Title.
     BX6333.P67517   1999
     252'.061dc20
                                          95-48119
                                          CIP

ISBN 1-573132-272-6

Contents

Preface to the Second Edition

Why doesn't God do more? At the distant horizon where the uneven ground of doubt meets the wide sky of faith, there is a cloud. The cloud on the horizon is shaped like a question mark. The cloudy question mark that hovers at the horizon works for a string of six very serious syllables: "Why doesn't God do more?" After all, we assume God can do more. So why not? If God cares, and if God can, they why? In the face of tragedy, disaster, violence, and disease, why doesn't God do more?

That question, or something similar to it, has been hovering around honest horizons for a long time. Once it was asked about Jesus—which lands pretty close to asking it about God. On the way to Lazarus' grave, some of the bystanders, seeing Jesus weeping with Lazarus' family, asked, "Could not this man who healed the blind have kept his friend from dying?" If Jesus healed others, why not Lazarus? If he cares, and if he can, then why didn't Jesus step in and spare Lazarus and his family this pain and grief?

That question is the substance of my most intense internal quarrel. William Butler Yeats once said that out of our quarrels with others we make rhetoric, but out of our quarrels with ourselves we make poetry. If one baptizes Yeats' wisdom, one might say that "out of our theological quarrels with others we make doctrinal statements, but out of our theological quarrels with ourselves we make quiet confessions."

Is Life Fair?

The words in *Is Life Fair?* are the leftovers of my quarrel with myself. They are the quiet confessions of one who has seen the thinness of "conventional wisdom orthodoxy" and a kind of religious optimism that can border on superstition. I have this long, unresolved quarrel inside of myself. It will no longer let me say some of the expected words I am supposed to say. In the face of the question with which I quarrel, "Why doesn't God do more?" I am left with the simple confessions that stumble about inside the walls of *Is Life Fair?*—timid attempts to say something livable, honest, and unadorned about the God who always does more than we can ever know, but who sometimes does less than we had always hoped.

—Charles E. Poole
Advent 1998
Jackson, Mississippi

Preface to the First Edition

In his magnificent poem "In Memoriam," Alfred Tennyson offered the insightful observation that "our words conceal as much as they reveal." Tennyson was absolutely right. Our words do conceal about as much as they reveal. That is true of words in general, and it is especially true of the words in this book.

The words in this book will, no doubt, conceal about as much as they will reveal, because they are clearing their throats to try and say something helpful and hopeful about life's toughest struggles, darkest tragedies, and deepest mysteries. Thus, given the rugged terrain over which these words will stumble, they are certain to hide about as much as they show, to conceal about as much as they reveal.

These words will not be perfect words that resolve all the bewildering mysteries. They will not be final words that settle all the difficult questions. Hopefully, though, they will be good words . . . good words for hard times.

When life is complex and hearts are broken and times are hard, we do not need words that are misty-eyed with shallow sentimentality, starry-eyed with naive optimism, or dry-eyed with cold logic. Rather, we need words that are clear-eyed with realism and wide-eyed with hope.

Those are the sort of words that have lined up to limp quietly across the pages that follow. They are not perfect words that dance with dazzling beauty, nor are they final words that strut with proud authority. They are, hopefully, good words—good words that will limp quietly into the broken places of life, clear-eyed with realism and wide-eyed with hope, the realism and hope that are the absolute prerequisites to an honest, livable, biblical theology for life!

These "good words for hard times" would not likely have had a book to travel around in had it not been for the kind encouragement of the wonderful people at Smyth and Helwys and the diligent typing of Christy Riley and Nancy Brannon. To all of them, for their help in bringing these words to "the light of day," I give my gratitude and thanks.

Of course, the words had to come from somewhere. I believe they found their way into my heart by the Spirit of the Lord our God, but I also know that they passed through many hands on their way to me.

—These words were colored and shaped by the influence of theologians and writers such as Henri Nouwen, Frederick Buechner, L. D. Johnson, Thomas Kelly, Kirby Godsey, and John Claypool.

—These words were lifted and blessed by living life, in good times and bad, happy and sad, at home with Marcia, Joshua, and Maria.

—These words were affirmed and embraced by the congregation of the First Baptist Church in Macon, Georgia.

—And these words were taught and given by a host of beloved teachers, the first of whom were our parents, to whom these words are offered in devoted gratitude on the page of dedication.

In his wonderful book, *Now and Then*, Frederick Buechner described his beloved seminary professor, James Muilenburg, with these unforgettable words:

> He . . . didn't or couldn't or wouldn't resolve, intellectualize, or evade the tensions of his faith, but lived those tensions out, torn almost in two by them at times. His faith was not a seamless garment but a ragged garment with the seams showing, the tears showing, a garment that he clutched about him like a man in a storm.[1]

With those riveting phrases, Buechner described, not only Professor Muilenburg, but you and me and all of us. We cannot intellectualize or resolve or settle all the tensions and questions and mysteries that surround such enormous issues as the will of God, the reasons for suffering, and the gift of prayer. God's ways are not our ways. We see through a thick glass, darkly. We cannot capture God in an orthodoxy, corral God in a theology, or corner God in a doctrine. Thus, our faith is no seamless garment, perfectly finished and finally hemmed. Our faith is more like what Buechner called "a ragged garment with the tears showing," a ragged robe that we clutch about us tightly as we live by faith into whatever storms life might bring.

The words that travel in this book try to talk about "the ragged robe" of an honest theology for life—an honest, livable, biblical theology for hard times; a theology that is born out of a theocentric view of life and a christocentric interpretation of scripture. (A theocentric view of life means you start with what you believe about God and *then* decide what you will believe about life's tragedies, mysteries, and problems. A christocentric interpretation of scripture means you interpret everything in the

Bible in the light of the best revelation of God we have ever had: the words and works of Christ. That doesn't put the four Gospels at the top of the Bible and everything else beneath them, but it does put the four Gospels at the center of the Bible and everything else around them!)

That is what the words in these pages are about. They will probably conceal about as much as they will reveal. They will likely hide about as much as they will show. They will not be perfect words. They will not be final words. But they will, hopefully, be good words for the weary ones who must stumble around on the rugged terrain of hard times.

If words were threads, then books would be robes. And if books were robes, then the one you are holding in your hands right now would not be a perfect, seamless garment. It would be more like a ragged robe . . . hopefully the kind you could wear to a hard time, the kind you could clutch about you in a storm.

—Charles E. Poole
September 1995
Macon, Georgia

Note

[1]Frederick Buechner, *Now and Then* (San Francisco: Harper & Row, 1983) 16.

CHAPTER 1

Strong in Broken Places

It is good for me that I was afflicted. (Ps 119:71a RSV)

We know that in everything God works for good with those who love him, who are called according to his purpose. (Rom 8:28 RSV)

And to keep me from being too elated by the abundance of revelations, a thorn was given me in the flesh, a messenger of Satan, to harass me, to keep me from being too elated.

Three times I besought the Lord about this, that it should leave me; but he said to me, "My grace is sufficient for you, for my power is made perfect in weakness."

I will all the more gladly boast of my weaknesses, that the power of Christ may rest upon me. For the sake of Christ, then, I am content with weaknesses, insults, hardships, persecutions, and calamities; for when I am weak, then I am strong. (2 Cor 12:7-10 RSV)

Do you remember your first job? Mine was as a construction worker. I was fifteen years-old. Minimum wage was $1.35 an hour. (If you lost your hard hat, they deducted seven dollars from your check. One week I lost two. When Friday came, after taxes and hard hats, I owed them money!)

Well, anyway, I was rather small for age fifteen, so the foreman usually gave me very lightweight jobs. But, one Monday when we had to pour the foundation for a house, some of the big guys were absent. Thus, I was given a battlefield promotion! The foreman told me to get one of those big wheelbarrows, let the concrete truck fill it up, and then roll the wheelbarrow over to the foundation form and pour it in. It all sounded simple enough. I eagerly grabbed my wheelbarrow and proudly took my place in line.

Everything went just fine until the truck operator actually put some concrete in my wheelbarrow. I took about two steps. The wheelbarrow began to swerve and tilt from side to side. It now weighed a lot more than I did. Try as I might, I could not right the ship. The wheelbarrow turned over and spilled the concrete in a big pile, right there on the ground.

I got up, picked up my wheelbarrow, and, in grave humiliation, returned to the line. (The worst was yet to come!) As I got back up to the concrete truck, the foreman uttered a few words with which I had previously been unacquainted, but that he felt were appropriate for the occasion of my return. Then came the worst embarrassment of all. He turned to the concrete truck operator and said, with a mixture of disgust and pity and loudly enough for all my colleagues to hear, "Load him light. It's him again! Load him light."

For a fifteen-year-old boy, nothing could have been worse. It's been twenty-five years, and I'm still blushing. "Load him light. It's him again! Load him light." As a teenager, nothing could have been worse, but, in the subsequent years, there have been times when nothing could have been better than to have somebody somewhere saying "Load him light." Haven't you ever wished that someone in charge of life would look down on you and say: "Load her light. She's already seen so much trouble." "Load him light. His life is already complex enough."

Many times I have yearned for someone to distribute the burdens evenly and make the loads light. I have long listened for the words "Load him light," but the last time I heard those words my shoes were gray with misplaced concrete, and my hair was black with teenage youth. Now my hair is gray, and my shoes are black, and I've yet to hear "Load him light" again!

The fact is, you and I are not promised light loads. (Occasionally, we need to ask ourselves, "What, after all, were we promised?" We sometimes tend to hold God to promises God never made.) God never promised us light loads. In fact, sometimes the loads are very, very heavy. The weight of life sometimes stoops our shoulders, slows our steps, and robs our sleep. God does not promise to insulate us from burdens and exempt us from sorrow. God does not promise to say "Load her light."

What God does promise us, though, is to always be with us, to always be for us, and to always wring whatever good can be wrung from life's heaviest burdens and toughest trials. I suspect that was the truth to which Paul was pointing in Romans 8:28 when he said, "We know that in everything God works for good with those who love God." Paul does not suggest, with a sort of "praise the Lord anyhow" glibness, that everything that happens is good. Rather, he says that, no matter what happens in our lives, good or bad, in all things God is at work to wring whatever good can be wrung from whatever comes into our lives.

Needless to say, the ultimate demonstration of that truth is the resurrection of our Lord Jesus. When God raised Christ from the grave, God brought the very best triumph from the very worst tragedy. That is the nature of God throughout the Scripture. It is God's nature to wring whatever good can be wrung from whatever happens in life. We hear that truth declared in Paul's affirmation that "in everything God works for good with those who love God." We see that truth demonstrated in the resurrection of Christ our Lord. And over and over again, we witness in our own lives, and in the lives of others, the truth that it is God's nature to bring goodness out of brokenness, joy out of pain, and blessing out of sorrow.

Is Life Fair?

We have all watched people go through great trials or severe trouble, only to emerge from the shadows stronger and better people than they were before their burden. So many times it seems that those who are broken by the hard twists and turns of life become deeper, quieter, and more sensitive and discerning than ever they would have been had they managed to skip through life unbruised by pain, unbothered by trouble, and untouched by sorrow.

As I ponder this notion of God wringing whatever good can be wrung from whatever comes to us in life, I think of the books, sermons, and poems that have most profoundly shaped my life and pointed me toward an honest theology of clear-eyed realism and wide-eyed hope. Most of those books, sermons, and poems were written by people who had passed through life's darkest valleys and borne life's heaviest burdens.

—*Tracks of a Fellow Struggler*, written by John Claypool after his daughter, Laura Lue, died of lukemia

—*The Morning after Death*, written by L. D. Johnson after his daughter, Carole, died in an automobile accident

—"Alex's Death," written by William Sloane Coffin after his son, Alex, died in an automobile accident

—"Sermon at Nathaniel's Grave," written by Frederich Schleiermacher after his son, Nathaniel, died at nine years of age

—The beautiful poems of that hill-country genius, Byron Herbert Reese, written in the ill-defined shadows of depression and tuberculosis

—"In Memoriam," the greatest extrabiblical poem in all the world, written by Alfred Tennyson after his friend, Arthur Hallam, died

—The stunning sonnets of Emily Dickinson, written in the darkness of disappointment, sorrow, and loss

On and on the list could go. Much of what is truest and best in this world was born in the womb of that which is saddest and worst. God, it seems, is determined to wring whatever good can be wrung from whatever comes into our lives.

I have found that to be true, even in my own relatively easy, mostly sunny journey. When Marcia, Joshua, and I went away to seminary (there was no Maria in those days!), I was a brash fundamentalist who thought he had all the answers to all the questions that mattered. I was much too sure about much too much! I had little patience with those persons who struggled with doubts or questions. I had little empathy for those who staggered along beneath the cloud of depression instead of bubbling over with the fountain of joy.

But then, a few months into our seminary days, I experienced a real brush with a melancholy shadow that I have since come to call "emotional paralysis." I learned, first hand, a little about depression. I learned, for myself, how it feels to sense that life is on top of you and to fear that you will never again get out from under it.

I lived through those days, obviously. I emerged from them, but I have somehow never left them behind. I can honestly say (without even enlisting the aid of those twin cheerleaders, hyperbole and exaggeration) that I have never been the same since. There is a sense in which I have never finished walking away from that darkness through which I passed fourteen years ago. I have, as they say, "never gotten over it," and I hope and pray that I never will, because God used that darkness to transform my life. I emerged from it with a quieter voice, a gentler heart, and a softer eye for the struggles and doubts of others. I went into that darkness strutting; I emerged from it limping. It is a limp I should hope never to lose.

I spent three years at the old Southeastern Seminary. I learned a lot in the critical light of the classroom. But what really made me into a minister of our Lord's gospel, I learned, not in the critical light of the classroom, but in the strange darkness of the soul's struggle. Whatever real worth I have as a preacher and pastor, I largely owe to a shadow through which I once passed and from which I have been limping ever since.

What the psalmist says is true: "It is good for me that I have been afflicted." What Paul said is so: God does wring whatever good can be wrung from whatever hard times may come into our lives. God is, indeed, strongest where we are weakest.

But it is right about here that we need to exercise extreme caution, lest we say too much. It is right about here that popular American theology has a tendency both to trivialize and to "over-theolgize" the truth that "in everything God works for good."

We trivialize this truth when we try to reduce it to some pithy little cliché that will fit on a bumper sticker or a billboard. You know, such phrases as "If life gives you lemons make lemonade" or "For every cloud there is a silver lining." Those little clichés are alright in their place, but they are utterly out of place when they are pressed into the service of the enormous truth of the gospel. This is a great mystery, the mystery of how "in all things God works for good with those who love God."

We trivialize that truth when we reduce it to a simplistic "sunny side of the street" exercise in "positive thinking." This is not starry-eyed optimism or misty-eyed sentimentality. This is clear-eyed realism and wide-eyed hope. This is the principle of the resurrection. This is the enormous truth that God is always at work in our lives to wring whatever good can be wrung from even the worst of life's hard times. We need to be careful, lest we trivialize great truth by dressing it in the ill-fitting knickers of popular folklore.

Not only must we beware lest we trivialize this enormous truth about God "wringing the good out of the bad," we must also be careful lest we over-theologize this truth by taking the popular next step that goes like this: "Well, if God used the tragedy or trouble to make you a better person, then that must mean that God sent you the tragedy or trouble so that God could make you better."

This view of life assigns everything that happens to the direct will of God. In this view of life, God is aiming problems at us, willing burdens for us, and putting tragedies on us in order to make us better people. This is popular theology, and, if we employ the pick-and-choose method of biblical interpretation in which we use a verse here and a verse there to assemble a platform, it is a view that can be supported with some scripture.

However, if you interpret the whole Bible with Christ our Lord as the measure of all things (a christocentric interpretation of scripture), and if you believe that God is as good as Jesus made God out to be, then it is a bit difficult to embrace the idea that God is looking down on people saying: "He's arrogant. I think I'll take his child and humble him down." "She's unkind. I think I'll send her a tragedy and soften her up." You cannot square that view of God with the words and works of our Lord Jesus. I believe that our Lord Jesus is the best look we have ever had at who God is, how God acts, and what God wants. Thus, I cannot even begin to believe that God is willing catastrophe for us, sending tragedy to us, or aiming trouble at us.

It is true that we often emerge from trouble and pain far better and stronger and more useful to God and others than we ever would have been without the trouble and pain, but that does not necessarily mean that God sent the trouble and pain. Trouble and pain come because we live in a world where there is trouble and pain. But when trouble and pain come into our life, God, who is always with us, is already there. And God, whose nature is to wring whatever good can be wrung from every situation, goes to work to resurrect something useful out of something awful. There is no need to "over-theologize" that truth by adding to it the idea that "if God used it, God must have sent it."

Our Lord Jesus often brought healing; he never brought disease. He often gave help; he never sent tragedy. I will let his life define my understanding of God, not as one who sends tragedy, but as the One who wrings whatever good can be wrung from the worst of life's hard times.

Tucked away in Ernest Hemingway's famous novel, *A Farewell to Arms,* there is the wonderful line that rings so powerfully true: "The world breaks everyone, and afterward, many are strong at the broken places."[1] Seldom, if ever, has a single sentence so fully embraced both clear-eyed realism and wide-eyed hope. "The world breaks everyone." That is the voice of clear-eyed realism. "And afterward, many are strong at the broken places." That is the voice of wide-eyed hope.

Sooner or later, life does break almost everyone. Very few people will manage to make it through life in this world unscathed by trouble, unbruised by pain, unbothered by disease, untouched by sorrow. Sooner or later, somehow or another, most everyone will bump up against some hard reality that will not budge or change or go away. Sooner or later, somehow or another, most everyone will be plunged into some dark night, baptized in rough water that is over their head.

When those difficult times come—and they will—we can decide to become bitter, angry, and brittle. Or, we can choose to open our lives to the presence of God, whose nature it is to enlarge us and deepen us and make us better because of what we have endured. It is, to some extent, up to us whether we will become brittle at the broken places or strong at the broken places.

Not long ago, I stumbled across a slender fragment of a tender letter that was written nearly a hundred years ago by an Austrian theologian named Friedrich von Hügel. It was a letter of encouragement that Mr. von Hügel sent to his niece, who was going through an extremly difficult ordeal.

Mr. von Hügel reminded his niece that there was no way out of her difficulty other than to just live through it. He told her that whether she endured those dreadful days bitterly or nobly, "they would still have to be lived through." He wrote that if she endured those difficult days nobly, seeking whatever was best in her trial, then the time would pass and she would emerge from it all a better person. If she chose to be bitter, however, the time would still have to pass, but the experience would diminish her and do her harm. Then, with these words, von Hügel concluded his letter to the troubled, struggling young woman: "I have now come to feel that there is hardly anything more radically mean and deteriorating than sulking through the inevitable."[2]

Those words from an uncle's letter to a niece in Austria would fit just as well in an apostle's letter to a church in Corinth. In one of his letters to Corinth, Paul said the same sort of thing to the Corinthians that Frederick von Hügel said to his niece:

> I have bumped up against something that will not change. It is inevitable that I will have to live with it. I have prayed repeatedly for God to fix it, remove it, change it . . . but God has said that the only way out of this is through it, not around it. It is inevitable, but I will not let it diminish me; I will let it enlarge me. God has told me that in my weakest and most broken place God's strength is greatest. Since I have to live with it and live through it anyway, I will let it make me better. I will not sulk through the inevitable; rather, I will let the place at which I am most broken

become the place at which I am the most open to God's presence.

Paul decided to open up his life to the presence of God, who is always and ever at work to make us strong, even (or especially!) in broken places.

We must come to terms with the fact that no life will be entirely free of broken places and heavy loads. The loads will not always be light. If we believe that because we are good or faithful or generous, then God is somehow obligated to load us light and keep us safe and spare us pain, then we are holding God to promises God never made. The fact is, the loads will often be light, but sometimes they will be heavy, and occasionally they will feel as though they are going to break us at the heart.

But even then . . . even when the load is so great that we find ourselves heartbroken by the unbearable weight of an enormous problem, even then, by the grace and goodness and power of God, we live. We actually live to laugh again. We live to actually live again. We live through things that, if someone had told us we were going to have to live through, we would have sworn we could not have done it. But we do live through those broken places, and, by the grace and goodness and power of God, we actually emerge from them better, kinder, wiser, and stronger.

By the grace and goodness and power of God, we limp across the rugged terrain of our complex lives, until our limping becomes its own dancing, because God is at work to make us strong, even (or especially!) in broken places. Amen.

Notes

[1]Ernest Hemingway, *A Farewell to Arms* (New York: Charles Scribner's Sons, 1929) 249.

[2]Baron Friedrich von Hügel, *Selected Letters*, cited in John Baillie, *A Diary of Daily Readings* (New York: Charles Scribner's Sons, 1955) 162.

CHAPTER 2

Loving God . . .
For Nothing

One day the heavenly beings came to present themselves before the Lord, and Satan also came among them.

The Lord said to Satan, "Where have you come from?"

Satan answered the Lord, "From going to and fro on the earth, and from walking up and down on it."

The Lord said to Satan, "Have you considered my servant Job? There is no one like him on the earth, a blameless and upright man who fears God and turns away from evil."

Then Satan answered the Lord, "Does Job fear God for nothing? Have you not put a fence around him and his house and all that he has, on every side? You have blessed the work of his hands, and his possessions have increased in the land. But stretch out your hand now, and touch all that he has, and he will curse you to your face."

(Job 1:6-11)

Shadrach, Meshach, and Abednego answered the king, "O Nebuchadnezzar, we have no need to present a defense to you in this matter. If our God whom we serve is able to deliver us from the furnace of blazing fire and out of your hand, O king, let him deliver us. But if not, be it known to you, O king, that we will not serve your gods and we will not worship the golden statue that you have set up."

(Dan 3:16-18)

Love bears all things, love believes all things, love hopes all things, love endures all things.

(1 Cor 13:7)

Is Life Fair?

When I was a boy, my father and I spent many Saturday evenings listening to classical music on the radio. Our favorite program originated in Nashville, Tennessee, 650 on your AM dial, brought to you live by Goo-Goo Clusters, Martha White self-rising flour, and, if I remember correctly, Doan's Pills.

Every now and then, the signal would fade out somewhere between Ryman Auditorium in Nashville and Edna Place in Macon. On those occasions, we would salve our disappointment by playing an album by our favorite orchestra: Lester "Roadhog" Moran and the Cadillac Cowboys.[1]

As their name would indicate, Lester and the boys tended toward the secular side of classical. They would, however, frequently lapse into a rather devotional mood, at which time they would call on their sacred repertoire, of which my personal favorite was a lively, but, nonetheless, substantive number called "They Would Not Bend, They Would Not Bow, They Would Not Burn."

This deeply moving piece was, needless to say, a musical setting of Daniel 3, the story of Shadrach, Meshach, and Abednego: They did not bend. They did not bow. They did not burn. And they did not say a whole lot, either. But when they did speak, they really had something to say, and what they said points you and me in the wonderful direction of loving God unconditionally . . . no matter what . . . for nothing.

When you catch up to Shadrach, Meshach, and Abednego in Daniel 3, they are in some bad trouble. King Nebuchadnezzar had built a big statue. He had passed a law that whenever the band struck up a tune, everyone was supposed to just drop whatever they were doing, fall down to their knees, and worship King Neb's statue—like it was a god or something.

But Shadrach, Meshach, and Abednego already had a God to worship—the living God of Israel. They were not in the market for another god. They were not of a mind to be bowing down to statues and kings and such. So when the snare drums rolled and bagpipes blew, they did not bend, budge, or bow!

Their refusal to worship the king's idol did not escape the attention of some of the natives who had been looking for some way to get these Jews. So off they went to the king and said, "O King, you passed a law, but Shadrach, Meshach and Abednego will not obey! You said that whenever the band strikes up a tune, everybody is supposed to bow and worship at the statue. But these strange Jews—Shadrach, Meshach, and Abednego—won't bend or bow or so much as tip their caps to the statue. They say they already have a god to worship, the one true God. They pay you no heed, King! They're ignoring your statue and breaking your law!"

Well, needless to say, all this did not set well with the king. So he had Shadrach, Meshach, and Abednego arrested and brought before him. He laid down the law to them one more time: "O Shadrach, Meshach, and Abednego, is it true what I hear about you? Is it true that you pay no mind to my band, give no heed to my law, and bend no knee at my altar? I'm going to give you one more chance. If, the next time the band plays, you fall down and worship the statue, then well and good. But if you do not fall down and worship, then . . . well . . . then you will be thrown into a furnace of blazing fire!"

And it's right about there that Shadrach, Meshach, and Abednego get their one speaking part in the whole story. The king has laid down the law, given them their options, promised them their punishment, and offered them a second chance. Now it's their turn. What they say to the king is one of the really great lines in the whole Bible: "O Nebuchadnezzar, we don't really need another chance to bow down at the statue, because that is something we will not do. Now, we understand the penalty. We know you're going to throw us into the burning fiery furnace. We believe that the God we worship can deliver us from the fiery furnace. We believe that our God can and will spare us from death. But if not, we still will worship our God and not your statue."

Shadrach, Meshach, and Abednego don't talk a whole lot, but when they do, they certainly say a whole lot. I do not wish to assign exaggerated significance to their words, but it seems to me that Shadrach, Meshach, and Abednego were saying that their allegiance to God was not contingent upon God's blessing or conditioned by God's protection. Oh, to be sure, they did say, "We believe that our God can spare us, protect us, and deliver us." But then they said, "but if not . . . but if our God doesn't bless us or spare us or save us from the fire, we still will worship only our God . . . no matter what."[2]

Here is the real pinnacle of the story of Shadrach, Meshach, and Abednego. Here is something that at least hints at unconditional love for God: "We believe that our God can give us the miracle we need. We believe that our God can and will bless us and help us . . . but if not, our God will still be our God." Their words are pregnant with a radical possibility—the possibility of loving God, not for something, but for nothing!

What a wonderful way to live! What a wonderful place to be! What a wonderful stance to take! "I will love God no matter what. I believe God can deliver me and heal me and help me. And I believe God will, but if not, I will love God no less, because my love for God is not contingent upon or conditioned by anything."

Hidden somewhere in all of this is the absolutely stunning notion that you and I might actually be able to come to the place in our lives where we can begin to love God unconditionally. The great gospel of grace is built on the enduring, abiding, astounding foundation of God's unconditional love for us. With that we are well acquainted, but here is something different.

Here is the idea that we, you and I, can actually reach a place in our lives where we love God unconditionally.

That sounds so strange, and yet it feels so familiar. It feels familiar because, while it sounds awfully ambitious to say "We can love God unconditionally," we know that it can happen. We know that it can happen because we have seen others who loved God unconditionally, and we have had our own moments when we ourselves have loved God absolutely unconditionally. We have known those glorious moments of unencumbered maturity when we loved God, not because we hoped to gain anything or receive anything or be blessed or spared or rewarded or protected, but only because we loved God for the sheer love of God and nothing else. We have had our glorious moments when we loved God, not for something, but for nothing at all but the love of God.

Tucked away in Frederick Buechner's book, *A Room Called Remember,* is a stunningly moving and strikingly powerful testimony that describes what it is like to love God unconditionally. It is a passage in which Buechner tells about the time he and his wife flew to a hospital on the other side of the country to be with their critically ill daughter. The Buechner's daughter was in her early twenties, but she weighed less than she had as a child. Her disease had reduced her to a skeleton. Buechner said that, though he had known her since the day of her birth, if he had passed his own daughter in the corridor he would not have recognized her.

Buechner wrote these words about what he felt at his daughter's side in that awful time:

> I had passed beyond grief, beyond terror, all but beyond hope, and it was there, in that wilderness, that for the first time I caught sight of what it must be like to truly love God. It was only a glimpse, but it was like stumbling on fresh water in the desert. Though God was nowhere to be

clearly seen or clearly heard . . . I loved God. I loved God because there was nothing else left . . . I loved God not so much in spite of there being nothing in it for me but almost because there was nothing in it for me. For the first time in my life, there in that wilderness, I caught a glimpse of what it must be like to love God truly, for God's own sake, to love God no matter what . . . I did not love God because I was some sort of saint or hero. I did not love God because I suddenly saw the light or because I hoped by loving God to persuade God to heal the young woman I loved. I loved God because I couldn't help myself.[3]

In these words Buechner describes what I would call loving God unconditionally. To love God unconditionally is to love God no matter what God does, or does not do, for us or give to us. This is the "but if not" kind of love that says, "Yes I believe that God will bless us and heal us and protect us and spare us. But if not, I am still going to love God. I will love God nonetheless, because I don't love God to get blessed or healed or spared; I love God for God's own sake. I love God because I can't help myself. My love for God is unconditional. It is tied to no expectation of any reward in return for my love. I believe God can bless me and heal me and protect me. And I not only believe God can, I believe God will. But if not . . . no matter what, nevertheless I will love God nonetheless."

That is the unconditional love that you and I can have for God. It is the kind of love for God that is so utterly unconditional that we not only do not love God any less if we are not blessed with good things, but we cannot love God any more when we are blessed with good things. Our love for God simply is not tied to any conditions whatsoever.

Across the years I have frequently heard said, and I am sure I have probably said myself, "Isn't God good!" when some surgery would go surprisingly well or some biopsy would come back clear and good, the implication being that God is good because our situation went well. But what if the surgery had not gone well or the test had come back with ominous findings? Would God be any less good? Is God's goodness somehow conditioned on how well things happen to go for us? The fact is, if the news is tragic and the results are awful, God is no less good. If the news is wonderful and the results are great, God is no more good.

What I am suggesting is that we can truly come to that place in our life where our love for God and our trust in God's goodness are utterly untouched and unmoved by circumstances. We can actually come to the place where we just love God for the sake of loving God, not because we think that there is something in it for us.

Remember the book of Job? In the prologue, God and Satan were talking one day, and God said to Satan, "Have you noticed my servant Job? What a guy! He's so good. He's so honest and kind. He worships joyfully and serves faithfully. That Job is one good fellow." Remember Satan's rather cynical, sarcastic reply? Satan said "I guess Job does worship you and do right. Look at how you've blessed him! Who wouldn't worship you if they were as healthy and wealthy as Job. Take away Job's health and wealth, and we'll see what Job is really made of. Surely you don't think Job loves you for nothing!"

Satan's assumption is that Job would not love God so much if Job didn't think there was something in it for Job. Satan's implication is that nobody, not even Job, ever loves God with an unconditional love. Satan's big question is "Does Job love God for nothing?" "Could it be," wonders Satan, "that Job serves God because Job suspects that serving God is the surest way to be rewarded with health and wealth?" Satan's question suggests that Job serves God for something, and that the something Job expects in return for his devotion is health, safety, protection, and security. With more than just a hint of cynicism, Satan asks God, "Does Job serve God for nothing?"

That question is manageable for us as long as it is about an ancient character named Job. But if you dust it off and ask it about you and me, it is almost more of a question than we can bear. Why do we do what we do? Do we love God for nothing, just because we love God, just because we are full of gratitude for God's grace and we couldn't stop ourselves from loving God if we tried? Do we love God for nothing? Or do we love God for something? Do we really believe, deep down inside, that if we give enough and do enough and serve enough, we can sort of get God in our debt, so God will be "obligated" to protect us and prosper us?

Must we love God for something? Or might we love God for nothing? Can we actually come to the place at which we love God with utter abandon, no matter what, no strings attached, unconditionally? Yes, we can; and, when we are at our best, we do! When you and I are most fully in touch with ultimate reality, we can honestly say, "Yes, I do love God for nothing. I love God unconditionally, no matter what. I love God for God's sake, for the sheer love of God."

Now think about this: It is when we love God like that, seeking nothing in return, that we are most like God, because that is the way God loves us: unconditionally. It is then, when we honestly love God unconditionally, that we can join in with Shadrach, Meshach, and Abednego and say: "Oh, yes. I believe that God can give us the miracle. I believe that God can and will bless us, heal us, and help us. But if not, I will love God no less. If no miracle or blessing comes, I will not be disenchanted with God or disillusioned by God, because I'm not loving God because I hope to be blessed or rewarded. I don't love God because I think there is something in it for me. I love God for nothing but the love of God!"

When you and I reach that place in our lives, we will be awfully near to the kind of love that Paul describes in 1 Corinthians. Paul says that "love bears all things, believes all things, hopes all things, and endures all things." That is how unconditional love looks and acts. Unconditional love never stops believing and hoping. When you love God unconditionally, you believe everything and hope everything. Even if you never see a miracle or get a special blessing, you never feel at all disenchanted with God, and you never stop believing everything and hoping everything.

And it isn't because you have that much faith; it's just because you love God with the unconditional kind of love that says, "I believe God can intervene and save and help and heal and spare. I believe God can, and I hope God will; but if not, I'll still believe and hope and love God nonetheless, because I just love God, and I'd love God even if there was nothing in it for me." This is the love that bears all things, believes all things, hopes all things, and endures all things. Maybe it is, after all, not our faith in God that causes us always to trust in God. Maybe, instead, it is our love for God that causes us always to trust in God, even when all the evidence is to the contrary.[4]

We can love God that way. We can love God unconditionally, no matter what. We can love God with the love that bears all things, believes all things, hopes all things, and endures all things. *We can.* We can come to that place in our life where we say, "I believe that God can spare us and protect us and heal us. I believe God can, and I believe God will. But if not, I will love God no less. I will believe no less and hope no less, because my love for God depends on nothing. I just love God . . . no matter what.

If the question is "Do I love God for nothing?" then the answer can be, "Yes, I do love God . . . for nothing but the sheer love of God. I serve God . . . for nothing in return. I give . . . for nothing. I am good . . . for nothing. Yes, I do love God . . . for nothing."

Oh, what a way to love! What a way to live! Loving God . . . unconditionally. Loving God . . . no matter what. Loving God . . . for nothing! Amen.

Notes

[1]The stage name "Lester (Roadhog) Moran and the Cadillac Cowboys" belongs to the Statler Brothers.

[2]For an excellent commentary on Daniel 3, see "Daniel" by Mitchell G. Reddish in *Mercer Commentary on the Bible*, Watson E. Mills and Richard F. Wilson, ed. (Macon GA: Mercer University Press, 1995) 712-13.

[3]Frederick Buechner, *A Room Called Remember* (San Francisco: Harper & Row, 1984) 42-43.

[4]Ibid., 21.

CHAPTER 3

What Judas
Did Not Know

When Judas, his betrayer, saw that Jesus was condemned, he repented and brought back the thirty pieces of silver to the chief priests and the elders.

> *He said, "I have sinned by betraying innocent blood."*
> *But they said, "What is that to us? See to it yourself."*
> *Throwing down the pieces of silver in the temple, he departed; and he went and hanged himself.*

(Matt 27:3-5)

For now we see in a mirror, dimly, but then we will see face to face. Now I know only in part; then I will know fully, even as I have been fully known.

(1 Cor 13:12)

Every time I think of Judas, I hear the haunting echo of Frederick Buechner's tender words. In his autobiography, *The Sacred Journey,* Buechner relates the tragic story of his father's suicide, which occurred when Buechner was a little boy of ten. Buechner tells how, several days after his dad took his own life, his mother found a farewell note that Mr. Buechner had scribbled to her on the back page of a brand new copy of a recently released novel called *Gone with the Wind.* The note said, "I adore you, and I love you, and I am no good."[1]

"I adore you, and I love you, and I am no good." Those are the words that Mr. Buechner left for his family. Concerning his father's tragic death, Frederick Buechner wrote these unforgettable words:

Is Life Fair?

> For many years, if ever anybody asked how my father died,
> I would say, "heart trouble." That seemed at least a version
> of the truth. After all, he had a heart. And it was troubled.[2]

If anyone ever asks us how Judas died, I guess we could say the same thing: "heart trouble." After all, Judas did have a heart. And it was troubled. In fact, Judas's heart was so troubled by guilt and shame and despair and self-hatred that, if Judas had left a note, it probably would have been identical to Mr. Buechner's: "I am no good."

As far as Judas could see, he was no good. As far as Judas could see, there was no hope. All Judas knew was that he had made a dreadful decision. All Judas knew was that he hated the way things had turned out. All Judas knew was that he hated himself.

But Judas did not know everything there was to be known. Judas knew only that part of the truth that he could see. There were things that Judas did not know.

What Judas did not know was that this terrible situation was not hopeless. What Judas did not know was that all was not lost, because God was not finished. What Judas did not know was that, despite his dreadful choices, he still had a future with God.

Judas was looking at himself, his life, and God "through a thick glass, darkly." All he could see was guilt and shame and despair. Judas could see no hope. Judas could see no relief. Judas could see nothing but guilt about his past, fear about his future, and despair about himself.

The Bible says that Judas went out and hanged himself. Beneath the suffocating weight of despair, Judas made the tragic choice to end his own life.

Judas is not a very popular subject with us. He forces us to think about one of life's most tragic choices. That is painful for us. But while it may be painful, there are at least a couple of things that the church needs to say and that people need to hear about Judas's death.

First, the church must say with compassion and courage that, while suicide is a tragic choice, suicide does not annul the grace of God. I am sure that the church meant well when, over the years, it indicated that a person who took his or her life could not enter into God's eternal presence. I really think that the church kept saying that in the hope that the threat of eternal damnation would deter people from the tragic choice of suicide. In the process, however, people who gave up on themselves, the future, and life were not deterred. In addition, their loved ones were left with the horrible sense that their parent or child or spouse or friend who had lived in such misery that they ended their own life was now condemned to everlasting torment for the last act of their life.

The church needs to have enough candor and compassion to tell the truth. Suicide is a tragic choice. That is true. But it is also true that a child of God's grace who, in a state of utter despair, ends his or her life is not separated from God forever. If committing suicide could cause one to "lose their salvation," then that would mean that the destructive act of suicide would be stronger than the saving grace of God. If that were true, then a tragic decision made in the last second of life could erase and annul a lifetime of walking in the light of God's love.[3] If someone who has been saved by God's grace can lose their place in God's kingdom and be eternally condemned on the basis of a tragic choice made in a state of despair in the last second of life, then I do not know God.

Let us tell the truth. Suicide is a tragic choice. But suicide does not annul the saving grace of God received by faith in the life of God's child. God's grace is greater than our worst choices.

Secondly, the church needs to have enough compassion and courage to say that finally, ultimately, no one can take responsibility for someone else's tragic choice. When someone we love takes their own life, the guilt we feel can be absolutely enormous. "Why didn't I see it coming? If only I had picked up on it. Why didn't I pay closer attention? Why didn't we get her some help? I could have stopped this from happening."

The fact is, the taking of one's own life is, finally, a physical act. No one has ever died from threatening suicide or dropping hints.

Please do not mishear me. We must be alert to the clues that a loved one is suicidal. We must take the suicidal threats and hints seriously. We must surround, with support, as much as we can, the one who appears inclined to suicidal despair. We must be vigilant and responsive. But, finally, we cannot take responsibility for someone else's tragic choice. That is a burden of guilt God does not intend for you to bear.

If you are carrying a load of guilt and self-hatred because someone in your life made Judas's choice, then you need to let go of that today. People do not stop breathing because we miss clues or fail to see signs. People die of suicide because they make a tragic choice and commit a physical act. You cannot take responsibility for someone else's tragic choice. You and I can no more take responsibility for someone else's actions than the other eleven disciples could take responsibility for Judas's tragic choice.

I imagine that when Judas chose to end his life, it was because he fell off into what felt like a bottomless pit of despair. Judas slipped down into what felt like a bottomless pit of despair because he was out of touch with ultimate reality. Judas must have been out of touch with the ultimate reality of life, the ultimate reality that he was not rejected or abandoned by God, despite his miserable decision to betray Jesus.

Judas must have been out of touch with the ultimate reality that our lives are not defined by our worst choices, our darkest secrets, or our biggest failures. Rather, our lives are defined by the fact that we are children of God's grace who are loved and valued by God despite our failures and flaws.

Judas must have been out of touch with the ultimate reality that from wherever we stand, we have a future with God.[4] We may be standing up to our neck in trouble. We may be stumbling up to our eyes in guilt. We may be floundering over our head in sorrow. But from wherever we stand, we have a future with God.

Judas must have been out of touch with the ultimate realities of life, the enduring realities of the grace and hope that are ours in God. He was so out of touch with those ultimate realities that he slipped down, down, down into the suffocating darkness of despair. Apparently, Judas could not see how things could ever be right or good or happy again. He saw nothing but trouble ahead. He could not see how life could ever be good, or right, or happy, or bearable again.

Judas based his whole life on what he could see, and what he could see scared him to death. All Judas could see was his guilt and shame and failure. But Judas was looking at himself and at God through a thick glass, darkly. There was other truth to see and other truth to know. But Judas missed it because he gave up on life, he gave up on himself, and he gave up on God. Instead of putting his life into God's strong hands, Judas took his life into his own hopeless hands, and Judas missed the future. Because he missed the future, he missed the resurrection of Jesus. Because he missed the resurrection of Jesus, he missed the triumph of God's goodness and grace over all that was evil, hurtful, and wrong.

If only Judas had waited, he would have seen the resurrected Lord.[5] If only Judas had waited, he would have found the joy of a second chance at life. If only Judas had waited, he would have seen that from wherever he stood, he had a future with God.

Is Life Fair?

From wherever you stand, you have a future with God. That is not a polyester thread of synthetic optimism to tie around your finger for hard times. That is not a spoonful of religious sugar to make the bitter medicine of life go down.[6] That is not a Sunday morning tune to whistle in the enormous darkness of pain and fear and despair. What it is, is the truth.

Hope is not sophomoric naiveté. Hope is not Pollyannaish utopianism. Hope is the ultimate realism. From wherever you stand, you have a future with God. No matter how ashamed or afraid or sick or confused or disappointed or depressed or weary or embarrassed you are, you have a future with God.

Several years ago I read about an interview between a major league baseball player from Latin America and a newspaper sports reporter. The baseball player was new to the States and had received only the slightest of introductions to the English language. He was asked by the reporter to name his one, single, favorite English word. He thought for a few moments and then said that his one, single, favorite English word was "youneverknow."

"You-never-know." Apparently, the newly immigrated baseball player had heard those three words linked together so often that he assumed they were one word. "You," "never," and "know" . . . they go together nicely and fit together perfectly. "Youneverknow" is a wonderful word. It is a word full of hope. It is a word pregnant with a future that is yet to unfold.

"Youneverknow" is the best word of all for those who must wait. After all, it is true. You never know what God will yet do.

So wait. Don't give up. Don't take your life into your own hands. Put your life in God's strong hands. You never know what good thing God will yet do. From wherever you stand, you have a future with God.

We know something that Judas did not know. We know that God raised Jesus from the grave. That tells us that with God, you never know what surprising goodness might finally emerge from the darkest darkness of life. So we wait, because we know something that Judas did not know.

If only Judas had waited. Amen.

Notes

[1]Frederick Buechner, *The Sacred Journey* (San Francisco: Harper & Row, 1982) 41.

[2]Ibid., 41-42.

[3]Source unknown.

[4]Carlyle Marney, *Pastoral Preaching*, Charles F. Kemp, ed. (St. Louis: Bethany Press, 1963) 65-72.

[5]For the phrase "if only Judas had waited," I am indebted to *A Pilgrim's Progress*, John Carey (Macon GA: Mercer University Press, 1980) 71.

[6]Frederick Buechner, source unknown.

CHAPTER 4

Medicine and Prayer The Ways of Healing Grace

In those days Hezekiah became sick and was at the point of death.

The prophet Isaiah son of Amoz came to him, and said to him, "Thus says the Lord: Set your house in order, for you shall die; you shall not recover."

Then Hezekiah turned his face to the wall and prayed to the Lord: "Remember now, O Lord, I implore you, how I have walked before you in faithfulness with a whole heart, and have done what is good in your sight."

Hezekiah wept bitterly.

Before Isaiah had gone out of the middle court, the word of the Lord came to him: "Turn back, and say to Hezekiah prince of my people, Thus says the Lord, the God of your ancestor David: I have heard your prayer, I have seen your tears; indeed, I will heal you; on the third day you shall go up to the house of the Lord. I will add fifteen years to your life. I will deliver you and this city out of the hand of the king of Assyria; I will defend this city for my own sake and for my servant David's sake."

Then Isaiah said, "Bring a lump of figs. Let them take it and apply it to the boil, so that he may recover."

(2 Kgs 20:1-7)

Is Life Fair?

As soon as they left the synagogue, they entered the house of Simon and Andrew, with James and John. Now Simon's mother-in-law was in bed with a fever, and they told him about her at once. He came and took her by the hand and lifted her up. Then the fever left her, and she began to serve them.

That evening, at sundown, they brought to him all who were sick or possessed with demons. And the whole city was gathered around the door. And he cured many who were sick with various diseases, and cast out many demons; and he would not permit the demons to speak, because they knew him.

(Mark 1:29-34)

On a cold December night in 1993, Marcia, Joshua, Maria, and I gathered around our kitchen table to light the candles on our Advent wreath, read from the Bible, and pray. Our scripture lesson for the evening was that passage in the Gospel of John in which Jesus says, "If you ask anything of the Father in my name, you will receive it." After we read the Scripture, we joined hands to pray by the flickering light of the rose-colored candle of joy. Our prayers were all focused on a friend of ours who was facing an ominous surgery the next day.

About an hour later, I happened to walk through our den, where Joshua and Maria were watching our weekly educational docudrama, "The Orlando Wilson Fishing Show." Maria, who was eight years-old at the time, looked up from the television and said, "Daddy, is our friend still going to have to have that surgery tomorrow?" I said, "Yes, dear. Why?" "Well," she said, "that Bible verse we read tonight said that if you ask in Jesus' name for God to do something, then God will do it. We asked in Jesus' name for God to heal our friend. So, if that's true, why will he still need the operation? Why won't God just heal him?"

It's a tough question. It is a grown-up question that just happened to be traveling on little-girl lips that night. But it finds its way onto other lips on other nights while we pray for healing, with all our hearts, in Jesus' name, to the background music of the rhythmic beeps and blinks of intravenous drips and intensive care artillery.

Where do medicine and prayer meet? How do the work of medicine and the mystery of prayer converge? If we get well, was it the work of medicine or the mystery of prayer, or was it both? Do medicine and prayer even belong in the same sentence? Can they both claim a place among the ways of healing grace?

An obscure corner of 2 Kings manages to herd medicine and prayer into the same corral. It is the intriguing story of Hezekiah's illness and recovery. Hezekiah's condition was critical. The outlook was so dismal that he was told to "get his house in order." In the face of such a bleak prognosis, Hezekiah began to pray for God to heal him. God then told the prophet Isaiah to go up to Hezekiah's room and tell Hezekiah that God was going to heal him and give him more years of life, despite the dark diagnosis and dismal predictions.

So Isaiah went up to Hezekiah's room and announced that God had heard his prayer and was going to heal him. In the same breath, however, Isaiah called for the attending physician to bring "a lump of figs" and put it on Hezekiah's sore so that, in the words of Isaiah, "he could recover."

So Isaiah is pronouncing Hezekiah healed by God, but he is also prescribing medicine for Hezekiah's illness. Isaiah assigns the credit for Hezekiah's recovery to the God who has heard Hezekiah's prayer, but he also says that the ointment made of figs must be applied to Hezekiah's sickness if he is going to get well —a sort of "say your prayers and take your medicine" approach to healing.

Is Life Fair?

In Hezekiah's case, medicine without prayer had not quite done it, but Isaiah seemed to think that prayer without medicine would not quite do it, either. So, while Isaiah was announcing that God's healing grace had come into Hezekiah's life through the channel of prayer, he was also calling for the science of medicine to serve as a means of that healing grace. "Bring a lump of figs and put it on his sore that he may recover." The "lump of figs" for which Isaiah called was obviously some sort of medicine. Whatever it was, apparently, it was the health care of choice for Hezekiah's sickness.

This is a seldom seen passage from the Old Testament. It doesn't get out much, but it might be helpful for us to dust it off. It seems to put the work of medicine and the mystery of prayer side by side, which, after all, is right where they belong.

The work of medicine, in its crudely primitive form then, and in its highly technical form now, is obviously a channel through which God's healing grace is brought to bear upon the lives of those who are sick and suffering.

I have a very high doctrine of the work of medicine. (I am not naive at this point. I know that the medical profession is no more immune from incompetence and insincerity than any other area of work. There is some incompetence and insincerity in every sphere of work, because there are a few incompetent and insincere people in every sphere of work. But, having said that, I do believe that those who work with competence and sincerity in the field of medicine are somehow near to the center of what God is up to in this world.)

Doctors, dentists, nurses, technicians, therapists, pharmacists, and all of those who labor with competence and sincerity in the work of medicine are toiling near to the center of what God is up to in this world. After all, God is on the side of healing, and the skills that medical professionals possess, properly used, frequently become channels through which God's healing grace can flow into a person's life. When their skills are used to diagnose and treat and comfort, then health-care professionals do somehow become instruments in the hands of the God who is on the side of healing and wholeness.

But what if the person in the lab or behind the mask or on the rounds does not believe in God? What if they are not inclined to confess that they are instruments in the hands of the God who heals? What then? Does God still use their skills as channels of healing grace? The answer, of course, is "yes." Every day, unbelieving doctors make correct diagnoses, perform correct procedures, and prescribe correct medications that lead to healing. So, does that cut God out of the process? No. Not at all. It simply means that the unbelieving person who serves in the work of medicine is a participant in a larger reality of which he or she is either unaware, or which he or she is unwilling to affirm.

But the truth is true, whether it is believed or not. Healing comes from God, and God uses the structures of medicine as channels of God's healing grace. If health-care professionals refuse to acknowledge that truth, then their refusal does not diminish their ability to participate in the process, but neither does their refusal to acknowledge the truth change the truth. The truth is always true, whether it is believed or not. But it is wonderful to see a doctor or nurse or technician or therapist or pharmacist or anyone in the medical profession who senses that their skills and abilities are somehow being used as channels through which the healing grace of God can be brought to bear upon a person's life.

The work of medicine, when it is at its best, is a channel through which God's healing grace flows into a person's life.

But, then, what about the mystery of prayer? Where does prayer enter into the process of healing?

Is Life Fair?

The witness of scripture joins with our own dearest experiences and deepest intuitions to affirm the truth that prayer is, indeed, a channel of God's healing grace. And yet, there is mystery. The mystery has to do with the fact that not everyone for whom we pray receives the good report or the full recovery or the additional years. We pray for some, and we see them get well. We pray for others, and we watch them grow worse. We had the same faith and passion in our prayers for both, but the results were not the same. There is mystery.

Needless to say, some persons will seek to dismiss the mystery with the simplistic answer, "Well if you had prayed harder or longer or with more faith, your prayer for healing would have been answered." I know that statement is a standard answer of popular American religion. But regardless of how many people are saying it, it does not quite ring true to the revelation of God in the life of Christ.

Is the God who is revealed in our Lord Jesus so reluctant to heal the sick that God must be begged into submission before finally healing the one we love? Does the God who is revealed in our Lord Jesus have some predetermined, but unrevealed, least minimum requirement of time and intensity that, if you do not meet, your prayer will not be answered?

To say "Everybody doesn't get healed because they didn't pray with enough faith or hard enough or long enough," is to answer one question, "Why doesn't everybody get healed?" with a quick, easy answer that raises a dozen darker questions about the very nature and character of God.

There is mystery here. You and I need to be honest enough to face up to the mystery, and we need to be humble enough to refrain from arrogantly claiming to have all the answers to it. Our problem is that we are so uncomfortable with mystery that we tend to prefer poor answers over no answers. But our poor answers have left many people disillusioned with God when the

34

quick, easy, poor answers broke down in the face of enormous realities that would not budge or change or go away, even in the face of the most ardent and intense prayer.

I cannot think about the mystery and wonder of the convergence of prayer and medicine without recalling those phenomenally insightful words of the late Harry Emerson Fosdick who said, "You can put off making up your mind, but you cannot put off making up your life."[1] Fosdick was so right. Never did a person speak the truth any more profoundly than that: "You can put off making up your mind, but you cannot put off making up your life."

That is exactly where I find myself on this whole matter of the work of medicine and the mystery of prayer. I have had to put off making up my mind about how medicine and prayer converge to serve as channels of God's healing grace. I have had to put off making up my mind about the mystery of why some are already well while others are still sick. I have had to put off making up my mind about why some have died but others have gotten the miracle.

I have had to put off making up my mind because all the mystery cannot be resolved. All the mystery is not resolvable because all the answers are not available. I will have to put off making up my mind. As the brilliant Baptist theologian Cecil Sherman says,

> It is unbecoming of you and me to claim to see through a glass clearly when no less a giant than the apostle Paul confessed that he could only see through a glass darkly.

I will have to put off making up my mind about how the work of medicine and the mystery of prayer converge as channels of God's healing grace, but putting off making up my mind does not mean that I must put off making up my life. In fact, you cannot put off making up your life. You have already made up your life, not around what you know, but around what you believe. I have made up my life too. Let me tell you what I have made up my life around concerning the ways of healing grace. It may help you, not so much to make up your mind, but to make up your life.

I have made up my life, first of all, around the truth that God is on the side of healing, wholeness, wellness, and health. I believe this because Jesus was on the side of healing, wholeness, wellness, and health; and the life of Jesus was the best look this world has ever had at who God is, how God acts, and what God wants.

When God decided to have a Word with us, the Word God gave was the life of our Lord Jesus. It is in that life, the life of Jesus, that we get our best look yet at who God is, how God acts, and what God wants. Thus, since Jesus went about bringing sanity, health, and wholeness to the troubled, diseased, and broken, I am sure that the God whom Jesus revealed is on the side of wholeness, healing, and health. I have made up my life around that. It is a place to start: God is on the side of healing, wholeness, and health.

When it comes to the ways of healing grace, I have made up my life around that truth. I have also made up my life around this truth: The science and practice of medicine is a channel through which God's healing grace often flows into people's lives. Just as Hezekiah needed the ointment made of figs, we need the antibiotic, the M.R.I., the chemotherapy, the surgery, the nurse's care, and the doctor's skill. These are to us what the ointment of figs was to Hezekiah. When it comes to the ways of healing grace, I have made up my life around the conviction that medicine and those who practice its science are often instruments in God's hands by which God's healing grace is brought to bear on our lives.

Beyond the science of medicine, there is something else: the enormous reality of prayer. When it comes to the ways of healing grace, I have "made up my life" around these truths: God is on the side of healing, medicine is an instrument of grace, and finally, to pray for healing means to tell God the truth and to trust God with life.

To say that prayer means telling God the truth and trusting God with life is to begin to see prayer more as a confession and less as a transaction. The transactional view of prayer is one that sees prayer as a transaction in which, if I offer God the proper currency of the right words and enough faith, then I, in return, can get God to come around and do my will.

This "transactional" view of prayer (though I would have recoiled from admitting it) was my own view of prayer for the first thirty years of my life. When I talked about prayer "working," I was talking about prayer as a transaction. The success of the transaction was measured by whether or not it "worked." Whether or not it "worked" was judged by whether or not I got the "answer" I sought.

That view of prayer, which is widely held and dearly loved by many wonderful people, is fine as long as it "works." As long as all the prayers are answered and all the sick are healed, the transactional view of prayer is fine. But what about when the prayer does not "work"? What about all those times when the "answer" does not come?

Then we have to start casting about for reasons, explanations, and causes. We say things like, "Well, sometimes the answer is yes, and sometimes the answer is no." But then, of course, we have to amend that by saying that sometimes when God says "no," God really means "wait." And then, of course, we have to wonder if God's "no" is really "God's no," or if we just did not pray long enough or hard enough or with enough helpers or enough faith to get God to say "yes" . . . and on and on and on it goes. The sad truth is, before long we have taken God's simple, beautiful gift of prayer and turned it into yet another test to be passed, riddle to be solved, and burden to be borne.

That is the grave liability of the transactional approach to prayer. It takes God's simple gift of prayer and turns it into a complex transaction that feels like another burden to be borne, another test to be passed, another riddle to be conquered. I know that view of prayer. I am intimately acquainted with it. I once lived with it as my own.

As I have grown in grace, however, I have come to "make up my life" around another view of prayer. This other view of prayer is what I call a "confessional" approach to prayer. It is captured in two phrases: (1) "Tell God the truth" and (2) "Trust God with life." Prayer as confession means simply telling God the truth that is at the center of our soul and then trusting God to do that which is best.

The ultimate example of the confessional view of prayer is the prayer of our Lord Jesus in the shadows of Gethsemane. On the night before his crucifixion, Jesus told God the truth: He wanted to avoid what he was facing if at all possible, and he said so. He just told God the truth that was at the center of his soul: "If it is possible, let this cup pass from me." That was the way Jesus prayed. He just told God the truth. The truth was, he dreaded what he was about to experience, and if there was any way around it, he wanted to find it. Jesus told God the truth: "Let this cup pass from me," and he then trusted God with life: "Nevertheless, not what I want but what you want."

That is the other side of prayer as confession: trusting God with life. Once Jesus had told God the truth—"If there is any way around this, let's find it"—he trusted God with life—"But if I have to go through it, then so be it. Not my will, but yours be done. My life is in your hands." In the garden of Gethsemane, that is the way Jesus prayed: telling God the truth and trusting God with life. He told God the truth about how he would like for his life to unfold, and then he just put his life in God's hands, not in fatalistic resignation, but in the quiet resolve that believes God can be trusted to do what is best.

In those dark midnight shadows of Gethsemane, I find the best picture of prayer as "confession" rather than "transaction." Our Lord Jesus, in the most intense hour of his life, did not treat prayer as a transaction in which he sought to convince God to "come around" and do what Jesus wanted God to do. In fact, if that was Jesus' approach to prayer in Gethsemane, then, for Jesus himself, prayer did not "work" that night. After all, the next day, he did "drink the cup." It did not pass from him as he prayed it ...ght.[2]

For Jesus in Gethsemane, prayer was not a complex transaction; it was a simple confession. He just told God the truth about what he wanted, what he dreaded, and what he hoped, and then trusted God to do whatever was best. That, for me, has become the ultimate model of prayer. To pray is to tell God the truth that is at the center of our soul and to trust God with utter abandon and quiet resolve.

If the truth at the center of our soul is that we are grateful for some blessing, then our prayer pours forth to God as a confession of thanksgiving. If the truth at the center of our soul is that we are awed by the greatness of God, then our prayer pours forth to God as a confession of praise. If the truth at the center of our soul is that we are bewildered by the suffering we face, then our prayer pours forth to God as a confession of dismay. If the truth at the center of our soul is that we are ashamed of some sin, then our prayer pours forth to God as a confession of guilt. If the truth at the center of our soul is that we are concerned about a missionary or a child or a stranger or a friend, then our prayer pours forth to God as a confession of intercession . . . and on and on the list could go.

But finally, to return to "the ways of healing grace," if the truth at the center of our soul is that we long for health to be restored to ourselves or to someone we love, then our prayer pours forth to God as a confession of need and desire: "O God, we need your healing grace because we want our father to be healed, our mother to get better, our friend to recover. O God, let the biopsy be clear, the surgery be successful, the tumor be benign. This is what we need. This is what we want."

That is the kind of prayer that pours forth from us in the face of serious physical illness, our own illness or the illness of someone whom we love. It is a way of praying that is captured in a line from the movie, *Shadowlands*.

Shadowlands is a dramatic retelling of the true story of the courtship and marriage of C. S. Lewis and Joy Gresham. Shortly after she met and fell in love with C. S. Lewis, Joy Gresham became ill with cancer. The remaining few years of her life were dominated by the advance of her disease, an insidious advance that was punctuated by occasional periods of comfort and remission.

During one of those "remissions" when Joy was especially mobile and strong, one of C. S. Lewis's university colleagues, noting Joy's renewed vigor, said to C. S. Lewis, "I know how hard you have been praying, and now God is answering your prayers." Lewis's reply to his friend constitutes a profound commentary on prayer as a confession of need and desire that pours forth from our lives. He said.

> That is not why I pray. I pray because I can't help myself. I pray because I am helpless. I pray because the need flows out of me all the time, waking and sleeping.[3]

In those words I hear a faint but true echo of what prayer for the sick has become in my own life: not so much a transaction in which I judge the prayer by what kind of answer I get from God, as much as a confession in which I simply tell God the truth and trust God with life—a confession of need, desire, and trust that pours forth from the center of my soul.

This kind of prayer is not the prayer we pray because "we ought to." Rather, it is the prayer we pray because "we have to." It is just as C. S. Lewis said in the movie, "We pray because we cannot help ourselves . . . The need flows out of us all the time." When prayer is a confession of need and desire, we cannot keep ourselves from praying, even if we tried. We pray, not because we ought to, but because we have to. We pray, not because we should, but because we must.

Our Lord's words to "ask, seek, and knock" cease to be a commandment about how we should pray and become, instead, a description of how we do pray. We "ask, seek, and knock," not because we assume that it is only by our persistence that we can get God to come around and give us what we want, but because we cannot keep ourselves from asking, seeking, and knocking. (I am convinced that our Lord's parable of the sleepy, grouchy householder who rises to help his neighbor only after being badgered into compliance is a story, not about "how God is," but a story about "how God is not"! It is a parable, not of comparison, but of contrast.) Our prayer pours forth from the center of our soul, not as a transaction, but as a confession of need and desire.

I found the magnificent freedom that this approach to prayer can give when Olif Hubert Poole was dying. Olif Hubert Poole was my father. He was diagnosed with liver cancer in November of 1993, and, by February of 1994, his oncologist estimated that he would live only about another six months.

There was a trip I wanted to take with my father. I wanted to take him to Kite, Georgia, to the Rehoboth Baptist Church cemetery to see, one last time, the graves of his mother and father. That little plot where Ma Bessie and Daddy Gene were buried had always been "holy ground" to him. I knew it would be an important and, indeed, sacramental act of closure for us to go back by that country church cemetery and then to walk around in the pastures and forests and fence rows where he and I used to go on those armed hikes we loosely called "hunting trips." I had intended to take him earlier, but I hadn't done it. Now I knew that I had only a few months in which to take my father to the places where he used to take me.

So . . . I prayed. I remember exactly what I prayed: "O Lord, please let Daddy feel well enough to take the trip to Kite and walk around in the fields and go by the cemetery." That was my prayer. It was simple enough, a prayer that my father would have one day that spring when he would feel like taking a sixty-mile drive and a leisurely stroll. That's all.

But that day never came. My father never felt well enough to go anywhere again. By March, he was in the hospital, and almost immediately he was in a coma. The prediction that he might live six months became the hope that he might live six days.

As I sat by his bed one evening, I came to terms with the fact that he and I would not be making our pilgrimage to Kite. But I at least wanted to be able to talk to my father one last time and tell him how grateful I was for the enormously powerful ways he had shaped and nurtured and blessed my life.

So . . . I prayed. I remember exactly what I prayed: "O Lord, I pray that you will let Daddy have a few more lucid moments, so that I can have that conversation with him that I really need to have." That was my prayer. It was simple enough, a prayer that my father would have one cognizant hour when he would be awake and we could have "the talk." That's all.

But that hour never came. He lay in a coma for four days, and, then, he died.

We never took the little trip I prayed we would. We never had the little talk I prayed we would. But right here is where I need to tell you something. Not once, then or since, has it ever entered my mind to say, "Well, my prayer didn't work"; or "Well, God didn't answer my prayer"; or "If I'd only prayed harder or longer, God would have heard"; or "If I'd gotten some other people to join with me in my praying, then God would have answered"; or "Why didn't God give me what I asked?"

Never once, not for a fleeting second, have I thought any of those thoughts. I no longer even have the capacity to think that way. I couldn't make myself think that way, even if I tried, because I no longer think of prayer as a transaction that must "work" or "be answered." Prayer, for me, has become something more akin to what I believe prayer was for Jesus in Gethsemane: a confession in which I simply tell God the truth and trust God with life.

Does that mean I have lowered my expectations of prayer? Oh no, not at all. Indeed my expectations of prayer have never been greater. In fact, if my father had suddenly awakened from his coma, healed and alert, I would not have been at all surprised. I would have been thrilled and happy, but not shocked or surprised. I am living in that second spiritual childhood, that post-critical simplicity that some theologians refer to as the "second naivete,"[4] so there is no mighty act of God in response to prayer that surprises me. My expectation of God's goodness, grace, and power is so high that, had my father awakened the moment I said "Amen," I would have been quite thankful, but not at all surprised.

On the other hand, when my father just lay there and died, I was very sad, but not at all disillusioned. I was sorry, but not angry. I had told God the truth and trusted God with life. So I took whatever gift God gave. In this case, the gift of God was death. I had my hands spread widely enough to catch whatever gift God gave because my praying was not about persuading God to do my will, but about telling God all the truth and trusting God with all of life.[5]

This is the understanding of prayer around which I have made up my life. I am convinced that it is somewhere pretty near to the truth about prayer. It isn't a neat formula that settles all the mystery. It won't fit on the same billboard that glibly announces "PRAYER WORKS." It is more akin to Paul's Roman affirmation that "we don't know what to say or how to pray, but God knows what to do and how to hear" (Rom 8:26-27, my paraphrase).

I pray for the sick to be healed, not because I should, but because I must; not because I am supposed to, but because I am compelled to; not because I have forced myself to pray, but because I can't keep myself from praying. My prayers for the sick are not transactional, but confessional. I tell God the truth and trust God with life.

When I say to the sick, "I am praying for you," I am saying: "The truth at the center of my soul is that I love you, and I long for you to be healed. When I pray to God, each day, the truth about my desire for you to be healed is the truth that will come out over and over and over again, pouring forth by day and by night."

Somehow, in ways that we will never fully understand, our praying becomes a channel through which God's healing grace is brought to bear upon the lives of the diseased and dying. God changes things, and prayer is one of the channels through which God's life-changing goodness, grace, and power find their way into the lives of those who long and yearn for wholeness and health. It matters that we pray for healing. It matters that we pray for the doctors and the nurses and the sick and the dying. The heart of God is not only somehow broken by our pain, it is also somehow moved by our praying. It matters that we pray. It matters more than any of us have ever known or even begun to suspect.

Around all of this I have "made up my life": God is on the side of healing, and medicine and prayer are both channels through which God's healing grace flows into people's lives. You can make up your life around that. It is clear-eyed with realism and wide-eyed with hope. It is simple, honest, and true to the witness of scripture.

There is much mystery around the ways of healing grace. The glass through which we see is thick, not thin . . . dark, not clear . . . complex, not simple. We do not know enough to make up our minds, but we do sense enough to make up our lives.

"We can put off making up our minds," said Fosdick, "but we cannot put off making up our lives." When it comes to medicine and prayer and the ways of healing grace, we can make up our lives around the truth that God is on the side of healing, and that when God's healing grace flows into our lives, it most always seems to travel through the channels of both medicine and prayer. Amen.

Epilogue

This chapter on medicine and prayer began to emerge in the winter of 1993, as I struggled with the terminal illness of a young, bright, dear friend. I am writing these concluding words twenty months later. It is August 14, 1995. I am sitting in a hospital room in Macon, Georgia, waiting for a surgeon's report. Marcia is having her second spinal surgery in less than eight years. She is young, bright, devoted, and good. She has lived with much pain for many days.

It seems both ironic and appropriate to write this epilogue on medicine and prayer while I sit in a hospital room, praying for my wife and for her surgeon. I have prayed for Dr. Hartman, that his skills and training will be used as channels through which God's healing grace can flow into Marcia's life. See, it's true. Not only on the stammering pages of simple books, but also on the rugged terrain of real life, prayer and medicine do belong in the same sentence. They do, somehow, converge. They are, both of them, the ways of healing grace.

Notes

[1]As quoted in John Claypool, *Tracks of a Fellow Struggler* (Waco: Word Publishing, 1974) 28.

[2]For an excellent commentary on the prayer of Jesus in Gethsemane, see John Killinger, *Bread for the Wilderness, Wine for the Journey* (Waco: World Books, 1976) 57-59.

[3]*Shadowlands*, screenplay by William Nicholson, Savoy Pictures, 1993.

[4]For the phrase "second naivete," I am indebted to Marcus Borg, *Meeting Jesus Again for the First Time* (New York: Harper Collins Publishers, 1994) 17.

[5]The idea of "opening the hands to accept whatever gift God might give" was spawned for me by a Wednesday evening prayer by Baptist theologian Richard Wilson.

CHAPTER 5

Is Life Fair?

Truly God is good to the upright, to those who are pure in heart.

But as for me, my feet had almost stumbled; my steps had nearly slipped.

For I was envious of the arrogant; I saw the prosperity of the wicked.

For they have no pain; their bodies are sound and sleek.

They are not in trouble as others are; they are not plagued like other people.

Such are the wicked; always at ease, they increase in riches.

All in vain I have kept my heart clean and washed my hands in innocence.

For all day long I have been plagued, and am punished every morning.

(Ps 73:1-5, 12-14)

For the kingdom of heaven is like a landowner who went out early in the morning to hire laborers for his vineyard. After agreeing with the laborers for their usual daily wage, he sent them into his vineyard.

When he went out about nine o'clock, he saw others standing idle in the marketplace; and he said to them, "You also go into the vineyard, and I will pay you whatever is right."

So they went.

When he went out again about noon and about three o'clock, he did the same.

Is Life Fair?

*And about five o'clock he went out and found others
standing around; and he said to them, "Why are you standing
here idle all day?"*

They said to him, "Because no one has hired us."

He said to them, "You also go into the vineyard."

*When evening came, the owner of the vineyard said to his
manager, "Call the laborers and give them their pay, begin-
ning with the last and then going to the first."*

*When those hired about five o'clock came, each of them
received the usual daily wage.*

*Now when the first came, they thought they would receive
more; but each of them also received the usual daily wage.*

*And when they received it, they grumbled against the
landowner, saying, "These last worked only one hour, and you
have made them equal to us who have borne the burden of the
day and the scorching heat."*

*But he replied to one of them, "Friend, I am doing you no
wrong; did you not agree with me for the usual daily wage?
Take what belongs to you and go; I choose to give to this last
the same as I give to you. Am I not allowed to do what I choose
with what belongs to me? Or are you envious because I am
generous?"*

So the last will be first, and the first will be last.

(Matt 20:1-16)

Well, what do you think? Is life fair? Yes or no? What do you say?
Is life fair?

Well, sure. Life is fair. The answer is "Yes, life is fair." Except
sometimes. Because sometimes, the answer is "No, life is unfair."
And then, of course, you have to factor in all those times when
life is better than fair.

So there is your straight answer to the simple question, "Is
life fair?" The answer is: "Yes." And "No."

First the "Yes," and then the "No."

Is life fair? Why yes, of course. You can see the fairness of life all around. And sometimes, the fairness of life is a beautiful sight to see. When life is being its fair self, it can be beautiful.

A husband and a wife have children whom they teach and nurture and love. They offer those children every affordable opportunity for education and development. The children grow up in that environment of nurture, take full advantage of those opportunities, and the parents watch with pride and joy as the children develop their gifts, graduate from school, and begin their own careers. There is a beautiful fairness about that: Good seed was sown, and a good harvest was reaped.

A family works hard, saves wisely, gives generously, shares graciously, invests carefully, and then lives long enough to retire and enjoy the fruit of their labor. The fairness of that is beautiful. They reaped what they sowed, and it was good.

Life can be very fair, and the fairness of it can be beautiful.

There is a beautiful side to the fairness of life, but there is also a brutal side to that fairness. Sometimes, life can be beautifully fair, but sometimes life can be brutally fair.

A person lives their life as a bitter, angry cynic, always looking for the worst in everybody and everything. One day they look around to discover that they have no friends. That is not a surprise. They have reaped what they have sown. And life is brutally fair.

A person embraces a sinful way of life. Then one day they discover that their actions have consequences. They begin to reap what they have sown. And life is brutally fair.

If the question is "Is life fair?" then sometimes, at least, the answer is "Yes, life is fair." And when life is fair, the fairness can be beautiful or brutal; because when life is being its fair self, what you reap is largely determined by what you sow, for better or worse. If the question is, "Is life fair?" then the answer is "Yes. For better or worse, yes, life is fair. . . ."

Is Life Fair?

. . . Sometimes. But what about when life is not fair? What about all those times when you seem to be reaping something you never sowed? What about when the answer to the question "Is life fair?" is "No." What then?

If you ever want to overhear someone yelling "No fair!" then just listen in on the seventy-third Psalm. Psalm 73 is one of the loudest cries of "No fair!" that we will ever hear.

The seventy-third psalm is attributed to someone named Asaph. Asaph is not one of your big-name Bible characters. We do not know a whole lot about Asaph, but what we do know about him is that he had seen an awful lot of life that looked to him to be dreadfully unfair.

Asaph's psalm is a fierce complaint about the unfairness of life. He has seen the wicked prosper and the good suffer, and he does not like it! Listen again to Asaph's complaint:

> I was envious when I saw the prosperity of the wicked . . .
> For they have no pain . . . they are not in trouble as others
> are . . . the wicked are always at ease. So for nothing I have
> kept my heart clean and washed my hands in innocence
> . . . for all day long I have been plagued, and I am pun-
> ished every morning.

Asaph lodges a double-barrel complaint. On the one hand, he sees good things happening to bad people, while on the other hand he sees bad things happening to good people, namely himself!

Needless to say, Asaph is not pleased with this bewildering unfairness. He goes so far as to say that he has lived a good life in vain and tried to do right for nothing. He has had some very hard times and some very bad trouble, while his irreverent and wicked neighbors, who do not so much as tip their hats to God, seem to be cruising through life on autopilot down easy street.

Something about this picture does not look right to Asaph. His psalm is thick with the echo of "unfair, unfair, life is unfair."

Who can blame Asaph? We sometimes feel the same way ourselves! We look around as Asaph did, and we are as bewildered as Asaph was. We are not troubled quite so much by the prosperity of the wicked as we are by the suffering of the faithful. Faced with the bewildering reality that some of the best people we have ever known are carrying some of the heaviest burdens we have ever seen, we sometimes say to ourselves, "It isn't fair."

Here is one of the most difficult corners for us to turn in our personal, spiritual, and theological lives. What is the answer to the apparent "unfairness" of the suffering of the faithful? I don't have all of the answer, and I wouldn't have too much confidence in anyone who claimed to. After all, "we see through a glass darkly." "We know in part," says the Scripture. I don't have all of the answer, but I think I know at least a part of it. At least a part of the answer to the unfair suffering of the faithful may lie in a new view of suffering that begins with a true view of God.

As long as we view suffering and disease and tragedy as something that God sends to us or puts on us, then the fairness/unfairness issue is just absolutely paralyzing. After all, if we envision God as purposefully sending tragedies to people or willfully putting agony on people, then that vision of God will eventually lead us to say, "God, you are not fair. You should not be devastating the dearest and best people by sending them the darkest and worst tragedies." As long as we see God as "sending" devastation to us, "putting" tragedy on us, and "willing" disease for us, then we can never get past the fairness/unfairness dilemma. And we will live out our lives quietly angry at God and secretly disappointed in God because God is, as Asaph complained, "unfair."

What we must do is to embrace a new understanding of suffering that begins with a true understanding of God. We must start with God, then figure out what we believe about suffering, rather than starting with suffering and then figuring out what we believe about God. We must not begin with what we think about suffering and then bend what we believe about God to fit our idea about suffering. Rather, we must begin with what we believe about God and bend what we think about suffering to fit what we know about God.

So begin with God. The best look we have ever had at God is in the life of Jesus, the incarnate Son of God. It is in the life of Jesus that we can best see who God is, how God acts, and what God wants. So, our understanding of God must be shaped by our encounter with Jesus. And where do we encounter Jesus? Well, primarily by reading the four Gospels in our New Testament.

If Jesus is the best look we have ever had at God, then, according to the four Gospels, what sort of God do we have? One who sends tragedy to us, wills agony for us, and puts devastation on us? That would not be my reading of the God who is best revealed in the words and works of Jesus our Lord. Go back and read the Gospels. The God who is revealed in the Jesus of the Gospels is the God who loves us enormously and hurts over our pain and is on the side of healing, wholeness, and health.

I read all four Gospels again this week just to make sure. You can read them for yourself. For me, the Jesus of the four Gospels reveals, not a God who is engaged in some cosmic exercise of "putting this on her" and "aiming this at him," but, rather, a God who is loving enormously, hurting deeply, and actively willing health and life and salvation for all people.

Now, since the revelation of God in the life of Jesus is the definitive starting place for me, then my view of suffering will just have to conform to my understanding of God. If God is as good as Jesus made God out to be, then suffering is not so much something that is sent, as it is something that comes. Mostly, suffering just comes. Why it comes does not cease to be a question, but it does fade far, far into the distant background.

Suffering comes because we live in a world where bad things can happen, and if bad things can happen to anyone, they can happen to me. (I don't like the sound of that. It sounds a little too random to suit me, but it is true to the biblical principle that "the rain falls on the just and the unjust.") Some of life's suffering comes, not because it was aimed at us or put on us, but because it came to us.

In the providence of God we are, no doubt, spared and protected from much that would hurt, harm, and destroy us. But we also know that we are not exempted or isolated from all of life's pain, else we would not have felt so much of it along the way. In the providence of God we are spared from some suffering. In the course of life, we are not spared from all suffering. When suffering comes, though, God is with us; and God is on the side of strength and healing and joy and life. That is the God whom we see revealed in the life of Jesus our Lord.

Go back and read the four Gospels. Do you see Jesus putting diseases on people? Do you see Jesus sending tragedy to people? No. What you see is Jesus on the side of healing, Jesus on the side of help, Jesus on the side of grace. If the life of Jesus is the best look we have ever had at God, then that must be the way God is. Jesus wept over the agony of his friends. Perhaps that must mean that God somehow aches over the agony that God's children experience in this life. I choose to believe that is true.

And thus, even though life sometimes looks awfully unfair, it never occurs to me that God is unfair. If I still believed that all this suffering was sent to us from God or laid on us by God, I might think God was unfair. But I am no longer willing to let my view of suffering determine my view of God. (That is a dangerously backward way to live!) Rather, my view of God will have to determine the way I look at suffering. And my view of

Is Life Fair?

God is shaped by what I have seen of God in the life of Jesus. That being true, I can say that while life is sometimes far less than fair, God is always far better than fair.

God has a way of loving us and blessing us that is so much better than fair. Think of the ways God has blessed us that transcend what we "deserve." Every good thing that has ever come to us is a gift of God's grace. If you and I could ever stop being self-centered long enough to be honest, we would have to say that we are not entitled to any good thing. We have no right to demand anything. And the last thing we really want is for God to just be "fair" with us. What we want and what we need is grace, the love that is better than fair. And grace is exactly what we ultimately receive from the God who is better than fair, even when life is less than fair.

If you want to see a single snapshot capture life being fair, unfair, and better than fair, then you need only to look inside the frame of that strange parable of Jesus' in Matthew 20. In that one parable, life feels fair, unfair, and better than fair. Inside the frame of a single story, life looks fair, unfair, and better than fair—all in the span of a single payday.

The story starts out fair and square. A farmer needs laborers to gather his crop. At six in the morning he finds some folks who want to work. They agree on a fair wage for a day's labor. The wage upon which they settle is fair. No one is displeased with the agreement. It is fair to all concerned. So the workers begin their day at six in the morning. *And life is fair.*

But that is not where the story ends. As the day goes on, the farmer keeps returning to town and recruiting other laborers to come and work. Some come to work at nine in the morning, some at noon, some at three, and, finally, a group is invited to begin work at five, just one hour before quitting time.

Here is where the story gets interesting, offensive, and even scandalous. It is time for the workers to be paid. You will remember that the first workers hired, the ones who worked the full twelve hours from six to six, had agreed beforehand on a fair wage for a full twelve hours of work. (What they agreed upon was a denarius. For sake of familiarity, we will say twenty dollars.)

Well, the farmer decided to pay off the workers in reverse order of when they came to work. So, the five o'clock workers he paid first. To everyone's amazement, he gave each of them, though they only worked one hour, a twenty-dollar bill. Then he gave each of the three o'clock crowd a twenty, and the same with those who came at noon and those who came at nine.

Well, needless to say, the ones who had started their day at six in the morning took due note of this stunning generosity. They thought, "Hmmm. He promised us twenty dollars each if we worked all day. So, if he gave twenty to all these others, even the late crowd that came at five, who knows how much he'll give us!" But when they got their pay, it was the same twenty dollars they had agreed upon early that morning.

As you might suspect, those all-day workers were livid! They converged on that farmer, crying the very same thing you and I would cry: "Unfair! This is unfair! We worked twelve hours. We've been out here sweating since sunup, and you paid us no more than you gave those latecomers who worked only one hour. No fair! This isn't right." *And life is unfair.*

But then the farmer answered them. In the farmer's answer we hear, not only the main point of the whole parable, but the main truth of the whole gospel. The farmer said, "Wait a minute. This morning, didn't we settle on what we all agreed was a fair wage for a day's work?" "Well, yes. But . . . " "And did I pay you what I promised?" "Well, yes, but . . . "

"Then what is your complaint? You got what you were promised. That is fair. If I choose to be better than fair with these others, what concern is that of yours? Can I not do what I want with my own money? Are you offended because I am generous? It's my money. I can be as good as I choose with what is mine. I was fair with you. If I choose to be more than fair with this late crowd, that is my business. Don't be angry because I am generous."

What a story! The late crowd goes home full of wonder at the gift of grace, the gift they did not earn but were given. *And life is better than fair.*

And there it is, captured in a single little story. In the parable, life starts out fair. Then, life looks unfair. Finally, life is better than fair. That is what the story is about. It is not about farming or economics or labor or wages. It is about how God can be as good as God pleases. It is about how God pleases to finally, ultimately give all of us more than any of us could ever earn or deserve or claim a right to.

There is a word for that kind of goodness, the goodness that is better than fair. The word is grace. And the truth is— ultimately, finally, when all is said and done—the last thing left will be the grace of God, the grace that will give us more than ever we could have earned or deserved.

Go back to the parable. Where in that story do you belong? I suspect that once life for us has ended and we have entered into God's unhindered presence, we will discover that none of us are in the early crowd who earned their place and deserved their pay. Rather, we will discover that every last one of us is in the late crowd who deserved nothing and were given everything. That's me, and that's you. We are all just children of grace. All is of grace, and grace is always better than fair.

I'm not so sure I want God to be fair with me and give me what I deserve, what I've earned, what I have a right to. I'll take grace over fair any day. And grace is what we get from the God of justice and mercy and love, the God who is better than fair. Amen.

CHAPTER 6

When It Isn't the Thought that Counts

What good is it, my brothers and sisters, if you say you have faith but do not have works? Can faith save you? If a brother or sister is naked and lacks daily food, and one of you says to them, "Go in peace; keep warm and eat your fill," and yet you do not supply their bodily needs, what is the good of that? So faith by itself, if it has no works, is dead.

(Jas 2:14-17)

Do your best to come to me soon, for Demas, in love with this present world, has deserted me and gone to Thessalonica; Crescens has gone to Galatia, Titus to Dalmatia. Only Luke is with me. Get Mark and bring him with you, for he is useful in my ministry. I have sent Tychicus to Ephesus. When you come, bring the cloak that I left with Carpus at Troas, also the books, and above all the parchments.

(2 Tim 4:9-13)

When I was a little boy, some well-meaning friend or relative would invariably give me the much disdained, but ever-present, handkerchief or socks for Christmas, instead of the much coveted, but ever elusive, ball or toy. My mother, in anticipation of that perennial blow of yuletide disappointment, would whisper in my ear on the way to the Christmas tree, her annual word of warning: "No matter what you get, say thank you. After all, it's the thought that counts."

Is Life Fair?

"It's the thought that counts." Those five words are frequently pressed into service at Christmas time, on birthdays, for Father's Day and Mother's Day, and any other time when gifts are given and presents are exchanged. Most of us learned that phrase rather early in life: "It's the thought that counts."

And it is true, not only about the gifts we give, but about the lives we live. Sometimes, in life, it is the thought that counts, because sometimes the thought is all we can offer or give. Sometimes there is nothing at all that anyone can actually do. In the face of great sorrow or deep trouble or enormous pain, sometimes about all you can do is take someone by the hand, look that person in the eye, and say "I am thinking about you. You will be in our thoughts and prayers." Sometimes, all you can do is remember someone in your prayers and save them a large place in your deepest thoughts.

Frequently, it is the thought that counts, because "the thought" is often the only gift we can give. We cannot reverse the tragedy, undo the sickness, fix the problem, hasten the grieving, or even lighten the load. So we can only pray for, and think about, our friends. In those times, we say that beautiful, magnificent, simple phrase: "I am thinking about you." And the thought counts. Sometimes, it is the thought that counts.

Having said that, we also know that there are other times when it is not the thought that counts, times when only real action and specific deeds can make a difference. In the little book of James, the message comes through loud and clear: sometimes it is not the thought that counts. James is, in fact, a bit blunt about it, isn't he? James says that if you can do something for someone and you do not do it, then, in that case, the thought simply does not count:

> What good is it, my brothers and sisters, if you say you have faith but you do not have works? . . . If a brother or sister has no clothes or food, and one of you says to them,

When It Isn't the Thought that Counts

"Go in peace, stay warm, and eat your fill," and yet you do not supply their bodily needs, what is the good of that?

James isn't difficult to interpret here, is he? James pulls no punches and minces no words. He says that sometimes it is not the thought that counts; rather, sometimes the only thing that counts is the deed. "If you're cold," says James, "all the nice thoughts in the world won't help. Only a jacket will make a difference. If you're hungry, all the nice thoughts in the world won't help. Only a plate of food will make a difference." James says that "if you see a naked or hungry person, your nice thoughts won't relieve their chattering teeth or ease their growling belly. In that situation, it isn't the thought, but the deed that counts."

For a practical picture of this principle, we need look no further than to a tender and moving passage from 2 Timothy.

Serious, devout, and reverent Bible scholars struggle with whether Paul himself or a younger follower of Paul's was the actual writer of 1 Timothy, 2 Timothy, and Titus, commonly called "the pastoral Epistles." That struggle arises from the fact that the grammar and style of the pastoral Epistles differ noticeably from that of Paul's other letters. Also, the organization of the church in the pastoral Epistles seems to be too sophisticated for the middle of the first century, when Paul lived and wrote. Suffice it to say that there are sound arguments both for and against Paul's authorship of the letters that bear the names of Timothy and Titus. Nevertheless, there is very little in the New Testament that sounds more like Paul than this poignant little corner of 2 Timothy:

> Do your best to come to me soon . . . and when you come, bring the cloak that I left at Troas, and also the books, and above all the parchments . . . . Do your best to come before winter.

Is Life Fair?

It is apparent from Paul's plea that he is in real need of some specific help. This is obviously one of those times in which it isn't the thought that counts. Paul is lonely, and needs some company. He is cold, and needs a sweater. He is bored, and needs a book. If Timothy had written back and said, "Dear Paul, I can't come and bring your sweater or your books, but I sure will be thinking of you," Paul would still have been just as lonely, cold, and bored. In this case "the thought" would not have counted nearly as much as a visit, a blanket, and a book. Paul needed specific help for specific needs.

Paul was in one of those situations that James described. Paul was in a spot where someone saying "God bless you, I'll be thinking of you" was not going to help a whole lot. Paul needed a friend to come, not a nice thought. Paul needed a sweater to wear, not a warm thought. Paul needed a book to read, not a caring thought. In Paul's situation, it was not the thought that counted. Only specific, actual, physical responses to specific, actual, physical needs would count for Paul in prison.

Please do not mishear me. Sometimes it is the thought that counts. Sometimes, indeed many times, our loving, caring, prayerful thoughts are all we can give. That is frequently true. And in those moments, the thought does count enormously. But sometimes it isn't the thought that counts. The poor cannot buy groceries with the money I thought about giving. The sad cannot find comfort in the note I thought about writing. The lonely cannot be cheered by the visit I thought about making. The discouraged cannot take strength from the call I thought about dialing.

Sometimes, it just isn't the thought that counts. Sometimes, there is no substitute for actually going ahead and doing what you are thinking. Sometimes the thought doesn't count a whole lot. Sometimes the only thing that counts is whether you actually obeyed the impulse, did the deed, gave the money, wrote the letter, made the visit, and lived up to the good intention.

Fred Craddock, that stunningly brilliant preacher who is now retired from the religion faculty at Emory University, once spoke about "the vast distance between the sky of our intentions and the earth of our performance."[1] That is a powerful way of saying that sometimes our actions just don't measure up to our thoughts. We often think great thoughts, feel strong impulses, make fine plans, and intend good intentions—only to stop short of actually doing anything.

Too often there is a vast distance between the sky of our intentions and the earth of our performance. Our intentions are way up there, but our performance is way down here. "We meant to" . . . "We planned to" . . . "We intended to" . . . "We thought about" . . . but we didn't ever actually get around to doing what we planned and meant and intended and thought. There really is a vast distance between the sky of our intentions and the earth of our performance.

Not long ago, I stumbled across a poem that seemed to capture something of this vast distance that looms like a canyon between the lofty sky of our good intentions and the flat earth of our actual performance. It is a simple little verse, written by a middle-aged man on the morning of his father's funeral. It is called "A Son's Regret," and it goes like this:

They nearly went and did things
More than anyone you know.
No father and son had better plans
They really meant to go.

They almost traveled many times
Down streams that don't quite flow.
They knew a brook where bluegill swam,
And really meant to go.

But one was young with work to do
While one grew old and gray.
And though their plans were all the best
They never found a day.

So they thought and planned
While seasons changed and left and slipped away.
And now, it seems, they will not go
Because one died today.

So the boy finally found the time
To spend outside with dad;
While they said goodbyes, in coats and ties,
To times they almost had.

A lot of life almost happens. A lot of life gets planned and intended and thought but doesn't ever actually get done. There is a vast, yawning canyon in our lives. It is the canyon of space that looms between the lofty sky of our good intentions and the flat earth of our actual performance.

Now please hear me. No person can do every good thing that crosses his or her mind. We cannot do every good thing about which we think. We will never fully, finally eliminate the distance between the sky of our intentions and the earth of our performance. We will all always think better and intend more than we actually get around to doing.

One of the most brilliant commentaries I've ever heard on all of that came from my old professor, friend, and mentor, John W. Carlton, who said to me back during my seminary days, "Chuck, boy, we're all going to die with half our music still inside." He was right. None of us actually lives up to all of our best impulses, highest intentions, and purest thoughts, if for no other reason than the limits of our time, energy, and money. We will all, inevitably, die with about half of our music still inside, with about half of our best impulses and finest plans and greatest intentions unacted upon.

When It Isn't the Thought that Counts

It's sort of like an acquaintance of Robert Louis Stevenson's said on the occasion of that brilliant writer's death. The admiring friend offered the wistful lament that "Robert died with a thousand stories still inside."[2] What was true of Robert Louis Stevenson is true for you and me. We will all die with a thousand good impulses unobeyed, a thousand small but helpful checks unwritten, a thousand simple but encouraging notes unmailed, a thousand quiet but uplifting words unspoken. That's life. That's the way it is. We will all die with at least half of our music still inside us—unsung, unsaid, undone. There really is a vast distance between the sky of our intentions and the earth of our performance.

But you and I must not allow all the things we have not done and cannot do to paralyze us with regret. Rather, we must decide to do our best to obey our highest impulses and to do at least some of the good things we have planned and thought and intended. If you and I wait until we can do everything for everybody before we do something for somebody, then we will never do anything for anybody.

And while we wait and think and intend, time goes by and life slips away. The young child waits for a trip that never gets taken. The aged parent waits for a visit that never gets made. The poor wait for a check that never gets written. The discouraged wait for a note that never gets mailed. The lonely wait for an invitation that never gets given . . . and life just quietly slips away.

So, what should we do, and how should we live? Well, perhaps we ought to begin by coming to terms with the fact that sometimes, the thought is the only thing that counts. Sometimes, all we can do is "think of someone." In those times, "it's the thought that counts," and it really does count. But we also need to remember that, as the book of James says, sometimes it is only the deed that counts. Those are the times we really need to go ahead and give the gift, write the letter, mail the card, dial the call, make the visit, order the flowers, spend the money, prepare the meal, give the food, speak the word, and take the time.

There will always be a vast distance between the sky of our intentions and the earth of our performance, because there will always be limits to our energy, money, and time. We cannot do everything for everybody. But we must do something for somebody; otherwise we will just mean well, intend much, and do nothing—while life quietly goes by, slips away, and ends.

Sometimes, it isn't the thought that counts. So do what you can. Because when you've done what you can, you've done what you should. Amen.

Notes

[1]Fred Craddock, taped lecture, Southern Baptist Theological Seminary.

[2]Quoted by John W. Carlton, *The World in His Heart* (Nashville: Broadman, 1985) 25.

CHAPTER 7

The Rugged Side of Easter

Now I would remind you, brothers and sisters, of the good news that I proclaimed to you, which you in turn received, in which also you stand, through which also you are being saved, if you hold firmly to the message that I proclaimed to you—unless you have come to believe in vain.

For I handed on to you as of first importance what I in turn had received: that Christ died for our sins in accordance with the scriptures, and that he was buried, and that he was raised on the third day in accordance with the scriptures, . . .

Now if Christ is proclaimed as raised from the dead, how can some of you say there is no resurrection of the dead? If there is no resurrection of the dead, then Christ has not been raised; and if Christ has not been raised, then our proclamation has been in vain and your faith has been in vain. We are even found to be misrepresenting God, because we testified of God that he raised Christ—whom he did not raise if it is true that the dead are not raised.

For if the dead are not raised, then Christ has not been raised. If Christ has not been raised, your faith is futile and you are still in your sins. Then those also who have died in Christ have perished. If for this life only we have hoped in Christ, we are of all people most to be pitied.

But in fact Christ has been raised from the dead, the first fruits of those who have died.

(1 Cor 15:1-4, 12-20)

Is Life Fair?

Something here looks a little out of place. I mean, after all, the *rugged* side of Easter? I didn't know Easter had a rugged side. I've never even seen the words "Easter" and "rugged" on the same page, much less in the same sentence. If Easter has a rugged side, it must be awfully small!

The only side of Easter I've ever seen is the exact opposite of "rugged." The fact is, if you take a look around, Easter actually looks anything but rugged. Easter, truth be told, has always looked sort of delicate and breakable and fragile. Think about it. Your main Easter colors are soft and pastel. Your primary Easter animals are tiny chicks and furry bunnies. Your traditional Easter flowers are gentle lilies and tender orchids. Then, of course, you've got your Easter bonnets, not exactly hard hats. And what about those ever-present Easter baskets? They are woven from little colored strands of straw to cradle the tender treasure of Easter eggs, lavender and pink and fragile as a whisper.

There is a long list of Easter things. All of them are delicate. None of them are rugged. That's the way Easter looks to you and me when Easter is busy being a day at the top of the year. When Easter is busy being a day at the top of the year, it is all dressed up in ribbons and bows. When Easter is busy being a day at the top of the year, Easter is delicate and gentle and anything but rugged. That's the way Easter looks when Easter is busy being a holy day at the top of the year.

But there is another side to Easter. Easter's other side is different from the delicate, fragile side we see when Easter is busy being a holy day at the top of the year. Easter's other side is a rugged, relentless, unbreakable side that waits, not at the top of the year, but at the bottom of life. It is that rugged side of Easter of which Paul wrote in his letter to the Corinthians. When we caught up to Paul in 1 Corinthians 15, he was staking his whole life on the rugged side of Easter that you can only see when

Easter, the day at the top of the year, becomes Easter, the truth at the bottom of life.

Paul had a whole other view of that which you and I call "Easter." Paul was as unfamiliar with the delicate side of Easter as we are with the rugged side of Easter. Paul was not familiar with Easter as a lovely day at the top of the year, but he was intimately acquainted with Easter as the rugged truth at the bottom of life.

Paul made it pretty clear that, for him, everything depended on the truth of the resurrection. He left no doubt that he was staking his whole life on the truth that God had raised Christ from the grave. (When it comes to what you and I call Easter, you might say that Paul puts all of his eggs in one basket!)

In fact, Paul went so far as to say that if there is no resurrection, if God did not raise Jesus from the grave, then there is no gospel worth preaching and no faith worth believing. Paul said

> If there is no resurrection of the dead, then Christ has not been raised; and if Christ has not been raised, then our proclamation has been in vain and your faith has been in vain. (vv. 13-14)

Paul went on to say that if Christ has not been raised from the dead, then we are found to be misrepresenting God, because we testified that God did raise Christ from the dead (v. 15). Then, as if all that were not enough, Paul added this:

> If Christ has not been raised, your faith is futile, and you are still in your sins. . . [and] those who died in Christ have perished. (vv. 17-18)

And finally, Paul pulled it all together in one last, grand, sweeping pronouncement: "If for this life only we have hoped in Christ, we are of all people most to be pitied" (v. 19). Without the resurrection, Paul says, life is pointless and we are hopeless.

Is Life Fair?

Paul has sort of an "all or nothing" attitude about the resurrection. He hangs the whole faith on a single peg. He stakes his whole life on a single truth.

Why would Paul assign such enormous significance to the resurrection of Christ? Why would Paul take the entire gospel and hang it on the single peg of the resurrection? Why would Paul say, "If God did not raise Christ from the grave, then our preaching is meaningless and your faith is useless and the gospel itself is empty, powerless, and futile"? Why would Paul go that far? Why would he say that without the resurrection, there is no faith to be embraced, no gospel to be proclaimed, and no hope to be trusted?

I think I know. I think I know why Paul put all his eggs in one basket, pinned all his hopes to one star, hung all his gospel on one peg, and cast all his trust on one truth. I think I know how Paul felt, because that is pretty much how I myself have come to feel. Many of Paul's words I do find strange, but not these words. Sometimes I find Paul hard to understand, but not this time. When Paul says that "without the resurrection we have no hope," it does not sound at all strange in my ears. In my ears, those words ring true. They ring true as the truest truth of all.

It rings true to say that the whole gospel hangs on the resurrection of Christ our Lord. After all, the word "gospel" means "good story." The good story of the gospel is that ultimately, finally, God will have the last word, and the goodness and grace of God will triumph and prevail over all that is evil and hurtful and destructive and wrong, and "the kingdoms of this world will become the kingdoms of our God and of God's Christ." That is the truth of the gospel, and the ultimate demonstration of that truth is the resurrection of Christ our Lord.

When God raised Christ from the grave, the goodness and grace and power of God triumphed and prevailed over all that was evil and hurtful and wrong. When evil had done its worse,

God did God's best. When God raised Christ from the grave, goodness and grace triumphed over evil and wrong. That is the resurrection, and the resurrection is the ground and source and reason for our undying, enduring, abiding hope that ultimately, finally, eternally, the same grace and goodness and power of God that raised Jesus from the grave will bring to pass that everlasting day when "the kingdoms of this world will become the kingdoms of our God and of God's Christ."

"But if you subtract that resurrection," says Paul, "then where is hope?" If you subtract the resurrection from the crucifixion, then what you have is the triumph of evil and darkness. Without the resurrection, the gospel ceases to be the "good story." "Without the resurrection," says Paul, "the reason for our hope is gone." "Without the resurrection," says Paul, "the ground of our hope is pulled from beneath our feet." "If there is no resurrection," says Paul, "then nothing else matters." Paul is right. His words make sense and ring true.

But once Paul has made his point, once he has made it perfectly clear that everything rises or falls with the truth of the resurrection, once Paul describes the emptiness and futility of life without the resurrection, then Paul says this: "But, in fact, Christ has been raised from the dead." After all that talk about how hopeless and pitiful we would be if there were no resurrection, Paul says "But, in fact, Christ has been raised from the dead."

And since Christ has been raised from the dead, the gospel is not empty, life is not pointless, and we are not hopeless; because if God raised Christ from the dead, then that means that God, not death, gets to have the last word. And if God is going to have the last word, then we can be assured that the goodness and grace of God will ultimately, finally, eternally prevail over all that is evil and hurtful and wrong. And if that is true, then that means that life really is not a bottomless pit of despair.

Is Life Fair?

That means that there really is a bottom to life, a bottom beyond which we cannot fall. And it is there, at the bottom of life, that you and I find ourselves caught and held in God's strong hands, resting ourselves in the truth of Easter, the rugged truth that puts a bottom to life and keeps life, even at its worst, from becoming a bottomless pit of despair.

When Easter is busy being a day at the top of the year, it is all ribbons and bows, eggshells and tulips. As a holy day at the top of the year, Easter is as delicate as a violet. At the top of the year, Easter is fragile and soft.

But at the bottom of life, Easter is something else altogether. When you hit the bottom of life, Easter is the most rugged, abiding, enduring truth of all. At the bottom of life, when you've fallen as far as you can fall, you bump into the truth that keeps life from becoming a bottomless pit of despair. At the bottom of life, there is Easter's truth: the rugged, unbreakable truth that ultimately, finally, God—not death or pain or sorrow—will have the last word.

Frederick Buechner, in a wonderful sermon called "The End Is Life," put it like this:

> Anxiety and fear are what we know best in this world . . .
> We have heard so much tragic news that when the news is
> good we cannot hear it . . . But the proclamation of Easter
> Day is that all is well . . . Love is the victor. Death is not
> the end. The end is life.[1]

That is the truth of Easter. It is always there, waiting for us, at the bottom of life. It is our rugged hope. Amen.

Note

[1]*A Chorus of Witnesses*, Thomas G. Long and Cornelius Plantinga, Jr., ed. (Ground Rapids MI: Eerdmans, 1994) 300.

CHAPTER 8

What Should We Say?

What then are we to say about these things? If God is for us, who is against us? He who did not withhold his own Son, but gave him up for all of us, will he not with him also give us everything else? Who will bring any charge against God's elect? It is God who justifies. Who is to condemn? It is Christ Jesus, who died, yes, who was raised, who is at the right hand of God, who indeed intercedes for us. Who will separate us from the love of Christ? Will hardship, or distress, or persecution, or famine, or nakedness, or peril, or sword?

As it is written, "For your sake we are being killed all day long; we are accounted as sheep to be slaughtered."

No, in all these things we are more than conquerors through him who loved us. For I am convinced that neither death, nor life, nor angels, nor rulers, nor things present, nor things to come, nor powers, nor height, nor depth, nor anything else in all creation, will be able to separate us from the love of God in Christ Jesus our Lord.

(Rom 8:31-39)

Then the seventh angel blew his trumpet, and there were loud voices in heaven, saying, "The kingdom of the world has become the kingdom of our Lord and of his Messiah, and he will reign forever and ever."

(Rev 11:15)

Is Life Fair?

Iused to say some things that I no longer say. Along the way, I have had to stop saying a few things.[1] Those things I used to say are not bad things to say. In fact, they probably help people to cope with some of life's most unmanageable problems. But I've stopped saying them because, for me, at least, they don't reflect the farthest reach and deepest truth of New Testament theology. Those sayings that I no longer say are not so much "untrue" as they are "not quite true enough."[2]

For example, when I first started out in the ministry, I used to say, in the face of pain and sorrow and loss, something like, "Well, you know God is in control, so even this must be God's will."

Assigning everything to the will of God is a reflection of that approach to life that feels compelled to defend the level of God's involvement in the world. I quit saying that everything was God's will, though, because I soon figured out, for one thing, that God does not need my defense, and, for another thing, that if I kept on saying that everything was God's will, then I was going to have to be willing to attribute to the will of God some things that were not only terrible and tragic, but violent and destructive. (After all, "everything" does mean every thing.) So, early on, in the face of tragedy, I stopped saying, "Well, God is in control, so this must be God's will."

I then started saying, in the face of tragedy, something like, "Well, this is tragic, but you know God makes no mistakes." I quit saying that, though, because, while I do ardently confess the perfection of God, if I invoke the phrase "God makes no mistakes" in the context of tragedy, then I am obviously implying that the tragedy is something God did. When I say, in the face of catastrophic illness or untimely death, "Well, this is tragic, but God makes no mistakes," then I am, by clear implication, saying "this is something God did."

I don't think I could go over to the Methodist church in Alabama where a tornado crushed the sanctuary on Palm Sunday of 1994 and ended the lives of little children who were waiting to put on an Easter pageant, and say "Well, God makes no mistakes." Does that mean I think God made a mistake in sending that tornado? No! It means I don't think God sent the tornado at all. Could God have stopped it? I am sure. Why didn't God stop it? I am not sure. Did God send it? I am sure not.

I don't think I could go out to Oklahoma City, find those whose loved ones died in the April 19, 1995 bombing of the federal building, and say to them, "Well, God makes no mistakes." Does that mean I think God made a mistake in sending that catastrophe? No! It means I don't think God sent the catastrophe at all. Could God have stopped it? I am sure. Why didn't God stop it? I am not sure. Did God send it? I am sure not.

Please hear me. I do not believe God makes mistakes. Indeed, God's perfection is the only perfection there is. But for us to say "Well, God makes no mistakes" in the immediate context of tragedy is irrelevant, at best, and misleading, at worst, unless we believe that God is directly responsible for the tragedy. If I say, "Well this is tragic, but God makes no mistakes," then the clear implication is that God is somehow willfully behind the horror. So in the face of tragedy, I stopped saying, "God makes no mistakes."

I then started saying, "Well, this is tragic, but God won't put any more on us than we can bear." For a while, I found comfort in that popular phrase, but a few years ago I had to put that one down, too, because of what it implies about tragedy and devastation and loss. It implies, of course, that God "puts it on us." And once again, you're right back to saying that God is "putting on" people all manner of violence and catastrophe.

Is Life Fair?

But what about 1 Corinthians 10:13? I know what it says.

No testing has overtaken you that is not common to everyone. God is faithful, and God will not let you be tested beyond your strength, but when you are tempted, God will also provide a way out so that you may be able to endure it.

I know that verse. I also know the larger context in which it appears. Its context is not about tragic suffering, but about temptations to sin.

I suppose, if we wish, we can conscript that Corinthian passage into the service of the phrase "God won't put any more on us than we can bear." I used to do that, but not anymore. Let me tell you why. If I come to you in your tragedy and say, "God won't put any more on us than we can bear," then I am clearly suggesting to you that God is purposefully putting on you the disease or tragedy that is tearing your life apart. But I cannot square that view of God with the Jesus of the Gospels. And since I believe that the Jesus of the Gospels most fully reveals the nature of God, I can no longer say phrases that imply that God puts on us, aims at us, or sends to us the enormous tragedies that devastate and fragment our lives.

Those are some of the things I used to say in the face of enormous pain and tragedy:

"This is tragic, but it must be God's will."
"This is tragic, but God makes no mistakes."
"This is tragic, but God won't put any more on us than we can bear."

I don't say those things anymore. They are not bad things to say. Many sincere people say them and find meaning in them. But I have stopped saying them, because, for me, at least, they don't reflect the farthest reach and deepest truth of the best, most sound, honest, biblical theology.

By now, you may be thinking, "What's the big deal? Who cares what we say? It's just semantics. They're just figures of speech. They're only words." But the truth is, it is by those kinds of words that people shape their view of God and life.

Several years ago, a lady from another city, upon learning that I was a preacher, began to talk about the death of one of her parents when she was only seven years-old. With quiet, but intense, anger she said to me: "You preachers are always saying that God has a reason for everything God does. Well, tell me, what possible reason did God have for taking my mama when I was a child and leaving us to struggle and suffer all these years?" I then had to say to her, "Yes, I am a preacher, but I don't say that. I don't say that 'God has a reason for everything that happens,' because I don't think God sent that tragedy to your family or to you."

You see, it's not just semantics. It isn't "just words" we are saying with all our popular religious clichés and slogans. Rather, for better or worse, it is theology we are confessing with all those familiar sayings we tend to say in the face of pain and sorrow.

What then should we say? Surely there is something to be said in the face of life's greatest struggles and heaviest burdens. Surely we are not just to fall silent and stare at the ground, mute and dumb in the face of sorrow and loss. Is there anything to say?

Oh, yes. There is something to say. It is not to be said glibly or trivially or lightly or with the doctrinaire swagger of those who think they have cornered all the truth and conquered all the mystery. But there is something to say in the face of tragedy and loss.

I can't tell you what you ought to say, but I can tell you what I have come to say in the face of tragedy and pain.

First of all, I have come to say what I believe Paul was saying in that magnificent passage from Romans. Romans 8:31-39 begins with Paul's question, "What shall we say about these things?" In answer to his own question Paul declares:

> If God is for us, who can be against us? . . . Of this I am sure, that neither death nor life, nor angels nor principalities, nor powers, nor things present, nor things to come, not height, not depth, nor anything in all creation will be able to separate us from the love of God that is in Christ Jesus our Lord.

What Paul says here is that "God is for us, not against us; God is with us, not away from us." That is what I now say in the face of tragedy and pain and death: Not, "this is God's will" or "God makes no mistakes" or "God won't put any more on us than we can bear," but "God is with us, and God is for us." In the midst of life and death, no matter what, God will never abandon us, reject us, forget us, or leave us. "God is with us, and God is for us." You can say that, and it always rings true, even in the deepest darkness of life.

And there is one other thing I now say in the face of tragedy, pain, and death. I say "God is with us and God is for us," because I am sure that is the truth that is tucked away in Romans 8. And I say something else. I say that "God will have the last word." I say that because of the truth I hear in Revelation 11:15. The entire book of the Revelation is captured in that one verse, which says "The kingdoms of this world shall become the kingdoms of our God and of God's Christ, and He shall reign forever and ever."

The book of the Revelation reaches its lofty climax, apex, and pinnacle in that single verse. The rest of the Revelation is a denouement from, an echo of, and a commentary on Revelation 11:15, "The kingdoms of this world shall become the kingdoms of our God and of His Christ, and He shall reign forever and ever."

For the original audience of this late first-century pastoral letter from Patmos, that meant they must not give up, because ultimately Domitian's oppressive kingdom would fade from the scene and God's goodness and grace would triumph and reign. For the rest of us, it means that ultimately, finally, all the hurtful "kingdoms of this world"—the kingdoms of evil and tragedy and oppression, the kingdoms of mental illness and emotional struggle and physical disease, the kingdoms of addiction and compulsion and fear, all those "kingdoms of this world" that conspire to hold us down and hold us under and hold us back—will be swallowed up into the kingdom of our God, and God's kingdom of goodness and grace will reign forever.

Thus, we can stare into the face of life's most awful moments and dreadful realities and say, with clear-eyed realism and wide-eyed hope, that "tragedy, while it is always real, is never ultimate."[3] If the kingdoms of this world are ultimately, finally, eternally, going to become the "kingdoms of our God and of God's Christ," then ultimately, finally, eternally, God, not tragedy, will have the last word.

God,
> *not cancer, will have the last word.*

God,
> *not depression, will have the last word.*

God,
> *not violence or racism or meanness, will have the last word.*

God,
> *not poverty, injustice or misunderstanding, will have the last word.*

God,
> *not paranoia or anxiety or despair, will have the last word.*

Not even death will get to have the last word. After all, this is God's world. And in God's world, it is God who gets to have the final say.

Is Life Fair?

God will have the last word. You can say that out loud, and it rings true. I am willing to cast my whole life on the truth of it. I am willing to, and I have.

So . . . what should we say? In the face of an inexplicable tragedy, a devastating loss, an incurable disease, or a heartbreaking death, what should we say?

I cannot tell you what you should say. I can only report to you, from the trenches and front lines of human suffering, both what I have unlearned and what I have learned.

I have unlearned the vocabulary that says:

"This is tragic, but it must be God's will."
"This is tragic, but God makes no mistakes."
"This is tragic, but God won't put any more on us than we can bear."

I have had to set that vocabulary aside. I have unlearned those lines. In their place, I have learned a new dialect of trust:

"This is tragic, but God is with us."
"This is tragic, but God is for us."
"This is tragic, but God will have the last word."

"What shall we say to these things?" asked the apostle Paul. And, ever since, ordinary folk like you and me have given our own uncertain echo to his question. We don't know "what to say to these things" when "these things" are too tragic for words.

Sometimes it is best to be silent. Often it is best to be speechless. Usually it is better to give an embrace than to offer an explanation.

But when the time does come to "say something," here is something we can say that doesn't say too much or too little. Here is something we can say that doesn't tell more than we know or less than we believe. Here is something that is clear-eyed with realism and wide-eyed with hope when we are wet-eyed with sorrow and red-eyed with weariness. Here are the most honest of all good words for the most awful of all hard times. Here is something that rings true, even in the darkest of nights:

God is with us.
    God is for us.
        And some day,
            somewhere,
                somehow,
                    some way,
                        God will have the last word.
                            Amen.

Notes

[1]This sermon was spawned for me by Scott Walker's *Life-Rails* (Philadelphia: Westminster Press, 1987).

[2]Fred Craddock, lecture.

[3]John Claypool, sermon.